WILDER WALES

WILDER WALES

Out and about
in North Wales
with
Ivor Wynne Jones

Wilder Wales

Copyright © Ivor Wynne Jones 2001

ISBN: 0-86381-696-7

*First published in 2001 by
Gwasg Carreg Gwalch, 12 Iard yr Orsaf, Llanrwst, Wales LL26 0EH
℡ 01492 642031   🖷 01492 641502
✆ books@carreg-gwalch.co.uk   Internet: www.carreg-gwalch.co.uk*

CONTENTS

PREFACE

These topographical explorations of more than a hundred villages, streets and buildings in North Wales (and one little-known corner of Wales in Belgium) were first written for the Liverpool *Daily Post*'s highly popular fortnightly series 'Out and about with Ivor Wynne Jones', which ran from June 1990 until July 1994.

Today's travellers will find many of the original newspaper cuttings preserved and framed in such places as church porches and friendly country inns where I found refreshment during my travels. They are here assembled in book form in response to a decade of letters and telephone calls from *Daily Post* readers, many of whom likened my personalised inquisitive forays to the pleasurable indulgences of George Borrow, midway through the 19th century, when writing his *Wild Wales*.

Each of the one hundred and eleven features has been updated as much as possible for the 21st century, but original interviews have been retained in the tense of the time, as tributes to those residents who so willingly co-operated, some of whom are no longer with us. Comments about such things as pub lunches found during my travels obviously relate to specific moments in the past. The time of the year might also be relevant to some of my original comments. To assist in the assessment of such comments the dates when the original versions were published are appended at the end of each feature.

This is an appropriate place to thank the countless people to whom I spoke during my initial travels for the series. Without exception each community expressed delight on finding it had been singled out for the *Daily Post*'s attentions. Many people took me into their homes to show me precious photographs, diaries, letters and other repositories of local information, much of which is now published in book form for the first time, to give it some degree of recorded permanence – thanks to

Myrddin ap Dafydd, of Gwasg Carreg Gwalch, in Dyffryn Conwy – the Conwy valley – of my paternal ancestors.

Llandudno 2001   *Ivor Wynne Jones*

ABERGELE

Churchyard teaser

ABERGELE was attracting summer visitors as early as 1795, when a surprised Englishman noted: 'They have a strange custom here that has an air of indelicacy to the stranger, which is that the inferior orders of people commonly bathe without the usual precautions of machines or dresses.'

Such uninhibited native innocence has long since vanished, for by 1808 another traveller, who described Abergele as 'a small mean town' was able to write: 'Of late years it is become a bathing place, in consequence of the general mania prevailing all over the kingdom for quitting home and every comfort for three months every summer, to experience all the miseries of contracted apartments. It must be very inconvenient for sea bathing, as it is a full mile from the sea.'

By 1824 it had its resident 'Betty the Bathing-woman', with her horse-drawn bathing machines, in which visitors undressed before being wheeled into the sea for minimum exposure to the world. Betty could never have imagined that her beach would be the scene of a vicious murder in December 1995, when a 40-years-old man was stabbed several times – the last victim of a notorious, serial killer.

Pensarn, the proper name for the bathing end, is a mile from the old Abergele, where the churchyard has a stone (possibly of the 17th century), bearing the strange Welsh inscription:

Yma mae'n gorwedd,
Ym mynwent Mihangel,
Wr oedd a'i annedd
Dair milldir i'r gogledd.

In other words, it is a memorial to a man born three miles to the north, which suggests he was born on land now lost to the sea, but is more likely to be a teasing reference to birth in a boat.

Some historic disasters are commemorated in the churchyard, like the grave of some of the one hundred and seventy-eight immigrants killed when the American ship *Ocean Monarch* caught fire in 1848, on her way out of Liverpool.

Here, too, are buried thirty-three people killed when the Irish Mail train crashed nearby and caught fire in 1868 – when notorious amorist Frank Harris (author of the once banned *My Life and Loves*), then only 12, gained his first experience of female anatomy, while helping a girl over a fence to watch the blaze. His primeval instincts ignited by the Abergele fire, they were inextinguishable for the rest of his 75 years.

A 21-gun salute was fired from the Vicarage garden in 1832 when the future Queen Victoria drove through the town with her mother, the Duchess of Kent, on their way home from Beaumaris Eisteddfod.

Between the church and the sea stands Pentre Mawr, best remembered as the home of Abergele Urban Council during 1935-74, and now tastefully converted into 24 flats. Its origins are uncertain for it was much altered in 1824 by the Jones (later Jones Bateman) family, who were said to have lived there for two hundred years. It was badly damaged by fire in 1850, and restored three years later.

Far more influential than Pentre Mawr was Bryngwenallt, built in 1867 a mile south of the town, for Liverpool-Welsh timber merchant John Roberts. As MP for Flintshire during 1878-92 he was the father of the famous Wales Sunday Closing Act, 1881, which survived in Dwyfor until the April 1996 reorganisation of local government. John Roberts was the father of the first Lord Clwyd. The family tomb dominates the entrance to Mynydd Seion Presbyterian Church, which they financed as an 1868 replacement for the original building of 1791, which stands beside it.

Unusually for a Roman Catholic church, I found St Teresa's locked. Although built as recently as 1934, it looks like a Byzantine structure transplanted from the Mediterranean –

14

thanks to its Italian-born architect named Rinvolucri, who lived at Glanconwy. He was not responsible for the 1971 interior alterations that some worshippers said spoilt the church.

(APRIL 1992)

ABER

The railway splash

The lyrically named village, Abergwyngregyn, near Bangor has been more commonly known as 'Aber' since the late Middle Ages. The Chester and Holyhead Railway Company arrived in 1848, and installed the short form in big carved letters on a tiny station half-a-mile from the village.

No one ever seemed to use the station, but it won international fame as the 'Aber splash'. After experimentation which began at Mochdre in 1860, the world's first water refuelling troughs were re-sited between the rails at Aber in 1871. They remained in use until 1962, showering the carriage windows as express steam locomotives scooped up water to enable trains to reach Holyhead without stopping.

Travellers who failed to look beyond the splash did not know what they were missing – and neither do those motorists on the modern A55 expressway who think there is nothing here but the Aber Falls Hotel, with the former University farm across the road.

Never much more than a hamlet, Aber grew out of a medieval community of camp followers, from the days when Llywelyn Fawr had a royal palace here. The location was significant in relation to the Beaumaris-Aber ferry, via the four miles of sand which dried out between tides, and across which Ynys Môn-bound travellers had to walk to meet the boat – with no hope of survival if the ferry failed to arrive before the tide.

This hazardous route to Ireland, along which countless people were drowned, remained in use until the opening of Telford's Menai suspension bridge in 1826.

Aber's ancient military mound, or motte, can be glimpsed between houses but is inaccessibly located on private land. Llywelyn's palace was probably on the opposite side of Afon Gwyngregyn, where some excavation was done in 1996 in the grounds of Pen-y-bryn, a 17th century house built in Elizabethan style.

Here, according to tradition, was where William de Braose seduced Princess Joan, wife of Llywelyn (and daughter of King John of England). 'What will you give to see your William?' asked Llywelyn. 'Wales, England and Llywelyn,' replied the Princess, whereupon Llywelyn opened a window to reveal her unfortunate Norman lover hanging from a gibbet.

Modern visitors to the hamlet are usually bent upon finding the spectacular waterfalls, some 1½ miles (2.5km) inland. There are spaces for about sixteen cars at the old bridge to nowhere – still known as Bont Newydd – where a cluster of notices guides the stranger to the public nature trail running through the trees of Coedydd Aber national nature reserve.

One of the notices says a guidebook to the trail is available from a house called Nant, a frustrating half-mile (800m) up the path. Having walked it I found the house closed for the winter. Subsequent enquiries at the Nature Conservancy Council offices in Bangor elicited that the pamphlet was out of print! Yet even without the benefit of the pamphlet there is a wealth of natural wonder to enjoy.

(NOVEMBER 1990)

AMLWCH

World's busiest copper port

AMLWCH grew around the picturesque creek which, by the end of the 18th century, had been converted into the world's busiest copper ore port. The reason becomes apparent if one takes to the air for a better view of the surrounding slopes of Mynydd Parys (*Parys Mountain*), and its rich pastiche of browns, reds, ochres, greens and blacks.

Those who have to remain at ground level can best see this bleak multicoloured landscape, topped with a derelict windmill once used for pumping, by travelling along the Llannerch-y-medd road. It will be noted that nature has made a valiant effort to reclaim this relic of 18th and 19th century exploitation of its mineral and chemical wealth, creating a Picasso-like view of the world.

To enable those resources to be exported, slabs of local stone were laid on end in the creek, in a dramatic exercise in dry stone walling, all neatly locked together and carefully angled, and looking as solid today as when the unique harbour was built.

Many of the old buildings have survived, including, somewhat surprisingly, one of the wooden chutes down which ore was delivered to the quayside, for loading into the ships. An old kiln has been dressed up into a stepped picnic area complete with dangerous hole some 8 ft deep, from which children should be kept well clear! A three-storey watch tower, at the end of an intermediate pier, bears an 1853 date stone. It was from here that a lookout would alert the harbour crews when an approaching ship needed some assistance while navigating into the harbour. The tower also served as a kind of lighthouse, providing a lead light for approaching vessels. These days the local trawlers and cabin cruisers rely on a distinctive lamp on a wall of the Adelphi Inn.

On the seaward side of what is known as Watchhouse Pier,

but still within the harbour, one can see the remains of a dry dock and adjacent boat-building yard. This picturesque scene is very different from the dull architecture in the town of Amlwch – a place that nevertheless offers an interesting stroll through streets which do little more than hint at the town's past glory as an international commercial and industrial centre. There is a good pay-and-display central car park, for those gifted with the intuition needed to find the amenity, hidden in a maze of one-way streets. However the amenities are not completed by the addition of public conveniences, which suggests that strangers are not expected. I did find some conveniences at the top of the approach road to the port, but they were firmly locked up.

Also locked up, as is generally the case in these troubled times, was the parish church, a strange structure designed by James Wyatt, built in 1800 and altered in 1867. I understand it contains 16th and 17th century memorials from an earlier church. The churchyard has been landscaped into a lawn, the paths being lined with the removed tombstones, bearing many interesting names.

(MAY 1994)

BALA

Father of the vernacular Bible

BALA has a broad and architecturally interesting High Street, of which much larger towns would be proud. Yet it began as 53 medieval burgage plots, stretching back to the parallel Heol y Domen *(road of the motte)*. The Norman motte is still there, a small defensive mound once protected by a ditch and concentric wooden palisades, and now a vantage point from which to admire the surrounding countryside.

Entering from the A5 one arrives at a cross-roads. To the right, is the former Calvinistic college founded in 1837. Outside the front door is a statue of founder-principal Lewis Edwards, seated with a book in his hands and others lying at his feet. Although erected soon after his death in 1887, the unusual design is a permanent reminder of the scandal which rocked the Presbyterian Church of Wales after the college closed in 1963, and its famous library was sold for a modest price to Richard Booth, the Hay-on-Wye book dealer who has since become equally famous.

Opposite the old Calvinistic college, a plaque on the wall of a large house reminds us it used to be a Congregationalist college, whose first principal (on another site) was the father of the Revd Michael D. Jones, founder of the Welsh republic in Patagonia.

That college's origins are recorded on a 1984 plaque, on a building opposite the Congregationalist chapel (1867) in Heol y Domen. This housed the college during 1842-69 – when Michael D. Jones succeeded his father as principal and chapel pastor.

To the left of the cross-roads a large car park is still known as The Green, once famous for its religious rallies and militia parades. Here, too, stood the Great Western Railway station from 1882 until 1965, when the link from England to Blaenau Ffestiniog was severed, to make way for Liverpool Corporation's creation of Tryweryn reservoir. The gorsedd circle on the Green is a relic of the 1967 National Eisteddfod.

As one enters the High Street the handsome restaurant on the left, called Neuadd y Cyfnod, is worth looking at. It is an 1851 restructuring of the grammar school founded in 1712. Its pupils included the novelist Daniel Owen, politician Tom Ellis, educationist Sir Owen M. Edwards, and his son, Urdd founder Sir Ifan ab Owen Edwards.

On the opposite side of High Street is Sir Goscombe John's magnificent statue of Tom Ellis, Liberal MP for Meirionnydd, 1886-99. The exquisite sculptures on the four-sided plinth are well worth looking at.

The town's more famous statue, to the Revd Thomas

Charles, is hidden away down Tegid Street, where it stands outside the Presbyterian Chapel built in 1866. Plaques on the front of Barclays Bank, in High Street, record it was where Thomas Charles lived during Mary Jones's famous visit after a very long walk in search of a Welsh Bible – the encounter that led to the 1804 creation of the British and Foreign Bible Society.

Largely unchanged, in or out, the Aran pyjama factory was a workhouse from 1841 to 1869, when it became a militia barracks. The Town Hall clock, installed in 1868, and once famous for being at odds with every other timepiece, now shows the correct time.

(MARCH 1994)

BANGOR-ON-DEE

Massacre of 1,200 monks

BANGOR-ON-DEE is best known for its racing, founded in 1859 as a two horse steeplechase to settle a wager between Lord Kenyon and Richard Myddleton Biddulph.

So many people turned up to witness the outcome that local farmers joined with Sir Watkin Williams-Wynn's Hunt to make racing an annual event, using the original course within a loop of the River Dee *(Afon Dyfrdwy)*. The course has been firmly established for more than a century as a place to pick the winners for Aintree, and some sixteen thousand people will turn up on a good day.

Bangor-on-Dee is just one of the many names for this rather upmarket village, that is best known to Welsh speakers as Bangor Is-coed (sometimes appearing as Bangor-is-y-coed), in a part of old Flintshire known as Maelor Saesneg, meaning English Maelor. Just to add to the confusion the notice outside the church tells us we are in Bangor Monachorum, an example of ancient Celtic-Latin tautology, for both words mean the same thing: a monastery.

The reference is to an old monastic community of enormous size. They were preaching a free-standing Celtic Christianity here long before St. Augustine landed in Kent in 598, to convert the pagan Anglo-Saxons to Rome.

In 601 Augustine was appointed the first Archbishop of Canterbury and Primate of Britain, a role which the Celts of Bangor refused to recognise, despite his travelling to meet them near Shrewsbury. Bede tells us this caused Augustine to engineer the massacre of 1,200 of the monks of Bancornaburg (as the Angles called it) by the Northumbrian heathen King Ethelfrith, in 613. About 50 of the Bangor monks escaped to set up the monastic community on Ynys Enlli *(Bardsey)*, where it survived as an independent order until the end of the 12th century.

No traces now remain of Bangor Is-coed monastery, and to that extent the parish church is a disappointment, though logic tells us 7th century farming monks could never have built anything very grand. Their faith however lived on, for there was a church here big enough for King Charles's troops to burn in 1644, lest it should be fortified by Cromwell's men. Repairs began in 1723, and four of the six bells, in the tower added at the same time, bear the date 1727, the others being 1811 and 1865. There were extensions in 1832, and the remains of the old chancel were restored in 1868 by John Douglas.

This was the church in which Douglas was married in 1860. He designed the Gothic choir stalls in 1868, and the pulpit in 1877. The organ screen is also his, but has been resited.

Next to the church is one of the world's most dignified and tranquil war memorials, in the form of an inscribed sandstone column, within a semicircular stone seat, in a garden on the banks of the Dee. From here one may gaze upon the narrow five-arch bridge nearby, and try to guess its age. It was in use long before Cromwell's troops crossed it, and could be medieval. It is still carrying traffic, but thankfully only in one direction.

There are two good inns opposite the church, and a mysteriously flamboyant gatehouse bearing the date 1897. It was the gift of the Duke of Westminster, marking the entrance to the 1868 Rectory.

(MARCH 1991)

BEAUMARIS

Journey to the gallows

BEWARE of the old church clock, if you should want to know the time while visiting Beaumaris which, as its medieval name reminds us, is a beautiful little town on the shores of the Menai Strait. The clock was cursed by Richard Rowlands, of Llanfaethlu, as he trembled his way to a public death on Beaumaris gallows in 1862.

While hangman Richard Calcraft prodded his prisoner across the town's bridge of death, to earn himself another £18, Rowlands proclaimed to the world that the church clock would for ever testify to his innocence. Oddly enough the four faces have shown different times ever since, and the clock's significance becomes instantly apparent to anyone who buys a ticket to follow in Richard Rowlands's last footsteps.

Starting at the town's 1614 Courthouse (used until the 1990s by local magistrates), modern innocents abroad can stand in the ancient spiked dock where Rowlands, aged 45, was found guilty of murdering his father-in-law, although there were no witnesses. He was ordered to be walked up the road to the local gaol, built in 1829, to be hanged by the neck until he was dead – the modern visitor's combined ticket also giving access to the gaol.

Seek out cell No. 22, on the upper floor. Seen from the corridor its only distinguishable feature is that the door has no Judas hole or feeding hatch. Internally the cell is found to be the regulation double size for its sinister purpose, to enable the prisoner to be accompanied at all times by two turnkeys, for whose comfort the cell was equipped with a fireplace.

Everyone sharing this particular corridor, in the north-west wing, would be conscious of its unique feature – the iron grille across an otherwise open doorway on the gable wall. The grille is directly opposite the gallows door on the outer perimeter wall. On execution days the gap was bridged, with the aid of supporting iron pintles which still form part of both walls.

Only on arriving at the grille does one see the church clock, peeping over the gallows door, to indicate the few moments of anguish left to prisoners crossing the bridge to eternity. With both grille and outer perimeter door already open, Rowlands could see the swaying noose from the moment he was marched out of his cell, his arms already pinioned.

Two clergymen described how he trembled as he walked the full length of the corridor, to the intonation of his own burial service. Prodded across the bridge by Calcraft, he stepped on to the collapsible shelf on the outer wall, to see the narrow street, 18 feet (5.5m) below, packed with jostling curious humanity.

He had to be helped to stand while Calcraft first strapped his knees and ankles together, and then placed the noose around his neck. A generation of Beaumaris people went to their own graves haunted by the shriek of the natives who watched the last public execution in North Wales.

On her deathbed, many years later, Rowlands's wife confessed to the murder, and there are still citizens of Beaumaris who shudder as they pass beneath the town's gallows.

Beaumaris gaol was designed by Joseph Aloysius Hansom, better known for designing the Hansom cab, and his name is still used for taxi legislation and regulation. He also designed some of the fine buildings in the town centre, including the Bulkeley Hotel.

Nearby Beaumaris Castle, built by Edward I (though never

completed), was the scene of earlier executions, notably of the priest William Davies, of Penrhyn Bay, hanged in 1593 and beatified by Pope John Paul II in 1987, at a special service in the Vatican, at which I was privileged to be a guest.

Beaumaris was where Lewis Carroll spent a childhood holiday in 1840, probably staying at the Bull's Head, which was then the post house – the rear coach yard having being converted into a restaurant in 1999. Carroll later celebrated his Beaumaris holiday in *Through the Looking-Glass* (1871) with references to Menai Bridge and the once-famous Beaumaris oyster beds.

In 1892 Beaumaris was found to have supplied the oysters used (several days later, without the benefit of refrigeration) to make a sauce which rapidly killed the Duke of Clarence, heir to the Prince of Wales, at a dinner in Colchester.

(JUNE 1990)

BERSHAM

Cannons for friend of foe

BERSHAM is a pretty little place, a surprising fact when related to its once dominant role in the European iron industry, including the manufacture of cannon for sale to friend or foe. Only about a mile from Wrexham's sprawling urban jumble, Bersham is a haven of rustic tranquillity, a hamlet of a dozen attractive houses wrapped around the preserved remains of its industrial past.

As surprising as everything else in Bersham is its ornate church, usually described as St. Mary's Chapel, having been built by the Fitzhugh family of the now-demolished Plas Power, which nestled in the trees above the hamlet.

The woods contain one of the best preserved sections of the eighth-century Offa's Dyke, built to keep belligerent Welsh warriors out of the border Kingdom of Mercia.

St. Mary's was built in 1873, and the tower was added two decades later. It was designed by John Gibson, better known for Bodelwyddan church and the old National Provincial Bank at Wrexham (and elsewhere). Still owned by Plas Power estate, it has regular services but is otherwise kept securely locked – as are the gates to the churchyard, which has been planted with exotic trees and shrubs instead of tombstones.

The name of Lloyd Fitzhugh, heir to Plas Power Estate, and a stalwart of the Royal Welsh Agricultural Society, appears on the unexpected liquor licence plate over the door of Mill Farm House, now a summer restaurant but built in the 18th century as the Accounts House of famous ironmaster John Wilkinson.

Beside it are two pairs of handsome estate houses, also the work of John Gibson, while across the road is Bersham Mill, an 1828 conversion of John Wilkinson's foundry. It was a corn mill, powered by a water leat which can still be seen at the rear.

An interesting octagonal brick building beyond the mill is Wilkinson's cannon foundry of about 1775, while the land between is undergoing archaeological excavation, which began in 1987.

Afon Clywedog runs through the hamlet, over a weir built by Wilkinson in 1779 to provide power for workshops that have long given way to farm buildings. Both river and road pass beneath the A483 Wrexham by-pass, which bisects the valley. Almost lost in the shadow of the modern viaduct is the half-timbered Bridge House, originally a group of five dwellings dating from the 17th century. It became the home of John Hawkins, manager of the ironworks in 1727.

The old village school, founded in 1842, rebuilt in 1874, and closed in 1961, is now the Bersham Industrial Heritage Centre, staffed by friendly knowledgeable ladies on behalf of the local council, and well worth a visit. It is at the centre of an enterprising network of country walks linking several aspects of local heritage made available by rare co-operation between local authorities and private individuals.

(JANUARY 1993)

BETHESDA

No more prayers at the chapel

BETHESDA town grew around Bethesda chapel, which is now closed and unkempt, and just another eyesore in a depressing High Street, with its broken windows and vegetation staining the unpainted walls of its once mighty facade.

Founded by the Independents in 1820, and replaced by the present structure in 1840, Bethesda is one of Wales's best-known chapels, named after the walled pool where Jesus told the cripple: 'Take up thy bed and walk'. The original Bethesda is still to be found within the Old City of Jerusalem. It is more than a century since Bethesda chapel's resident organist, R.S. Hughes, was composing tunes like *'Arafa Don'* and *'Y Dymhestl'*, which are still highly popular on the Welsh concert platform.

Across the road the former Baptist chapel is now a workshop, of which one resident said: 'At least it is serving some useful purpose'. I was unable to find anyone who remembered its name (Tabernacle).

Siloam Wesleyan Methodist chapel, built in 1872, has been demolished, but Jerusalem Calvinistic Methodist chapel, dating from 1890, still functions, as does the starkly functional Glan Ogwen or Christ Church, built for the Anglicans in 1856, to one of the poorest designs of the prolific Thomas H. Wyatt, always a little deficient in his aesthetic values. The church is surrounded by a forest of enormous purple gravestones, their size indicative of the slate opulence on which Bethesda grew, to house the workers at Penrhyn quarry. At its peak the quarry employed about three thousand men, extracting roofing slate from the world's biggest man-made hole. Now the figure is around one hundred and seventy in a very depressed building market.

Bethesda's decline began in April 1900, when, in an attempt to prevent coercion, the management banned the collection of trade union subscriptions on quarry premises. The resultant ill-feeling led to assaults on non-union men, dismissal of the ringleaders, and an Army cordon for subsequent prosecutions at Bangor magistrates court. When management closed some of the galleries in November the men stopped work for an explanation. The manager told them either to resume work or leave the premises quietly, and out they went – for the next three years, and the most famous strike in Welsh history. By the time the men returned to the quarry the international building trade had found alternatives for the slates which Penrhyn could not supply, and Bethesda has been dying ever since.

High above the narrow High Street (which is also the old A5 road London-Holyhead) there is a useful car park from where one can look over the roofs to the quarry beyond. On the skyline, north of the man-made mountain of slate waste, there is the spire of St. Ann's church, posing some interesting thoughts for hagiographers, who know that in Jerusalem the church dedicated to Ann, mother of the Virgin Mary, is also beside Bethesda.

It was fortuitous for Lord Penrhyn that there was a saint to match the name of his wife when he gave the community a church in 1813. That church now lies buried in slate waste but the name was preserved in its 1865 replacement.

(MARCH 1993)

BETWS-YN-RHOS

A perfect village.

BETWS-YN-RHOS is as near a perfect village as one could ever expect to find, though straddling a couple of horrendous bends never intended for modern traffic.

Once astride the main road from Chester to Conwy ferry, the village has retained its reputation as an ideal refreshment stop. The Wheatsheaf was the official coaching stop during the 18th century, though the building is much older. Its present name is derived from the coat of arms of the Oldfield family, who lived at Ffarm, the big manor house to the rear, which is now a rival restaurant. The Wheatsheaf used to be licensed as the Beehive, though known locally simply as Dafarn Uchaf *(Upper Tavern)* to distinguish it from Dafarn Isaf *(Lower Tavern)* at the bottom of the hill.

Equally old, Dafarn Isaf was licensed as the Saracen's Head, Saracen often being a polite neighbourly mutation from an armorial feature which began as a Saxon's head during the wars between the Welsh and the English.

More recently Dafarn Isaf was known as Llais Afon, where Myfi Williams, a former nurse gave Betws-yn-Rhos an enviable catering reputation during her 16-year incumbency, from which she retired some years ago. The inn subsequently closed but the singing river still runs past it and under the main street, the general consensus being that its name is probably Afon Fedw.

Despite the traffic hazards, modern motor coaches visit the village in the summer for tourists to watch the hour being struck on the dual-purpose church bell, suspended between two mini-towers over the western entrance. A quixotic creation of John Welch, and looking like a poor man's do-it-yourself Neuschwanstein, the belfry-cum-clocktower is served both by a tolling rope and a complex hinged mechanism linked to the clock – which keeps time.

Built in 1838, the church still displays its seating plan in the porch, to provide an interesting social study. The Coed Coch and Ffarm families glowered at each other from inward facing pews on either side of the tiny chancel, with their respective servants in the front rows of the forward facing pews. In the Victorian pecking order the Vicarage family were seated two rows behind the Coed Coch servants, and the Vicarage servants yet a further seven rows to the rear.

The church's east window is inscribed in memory of Mary (died 1844), wife of John Wynn, of Coed Coch (not to be confused with Mary, wife of John Lloyd Wynn, of Coed Coch, son of Mary). Coed Coch estate earned international fame with its stud of Welsh ponies which was dispersed in 1978, on the death of Miss Margaret 'Daisy' Brodrick.

Coed Coch became known as Living Waters in 1980, being a Christian centre for residential courses, or simply for group use as a base for exploring the countryside, but it closed in 1999. Before that it was known as Heronwater School, where Dr Fisher, the then Archbishop of Canterbury, used to spend his summer holidays in the 1950s, wearing non-clerical casual clothing. He preferred to worship at Llanelian church, occupying the seat beneath the pulpit, to the dismay of the then incumbent.

Betws-yn-Rhos was the birthplace, in 1871 (at Gwyndy Ucha) of journalist, author and poet Professor T. Gwynn Jones. He had little formal education but was a natural writer and spent 19 years in journalism before becoming a cataloguer at the National Library of Wales, from where he moved into the academic world as professor of Welsh literature, at Aberystwyth, in 1919.

(APRIL 1993)

BODELWYDDAN

A splendid folly

BODELWYDDAN Castle is an outpost of London's National Portrait Gallery, a role that surprises visitors in search of a stately home. Little remains of whatever imprint the Williams family made inside their romantic castle, whose turrets and battlements were added during 1830-36 around a house they had owned since the 17th century. They removed almost everything before selling the house in 1920 to Lowther College, whose girls occupied it until 1962. When the then Clwyd County Council bought it in 1983 the interior had been repainted to match the utilitarian needs of the pupils. The castle is now administered by the Bodelwyddan Museum Trustees.

Today's visitor sees how a Victorian house of this size might have looked – if modern interior designer Roderick Gradidge had been available. The result is a splendid folly, both inside and out, and there is a lot to be said for viewing it merely as an art gallery, housing a remarkably rich collection of 19th century portraits and borrowed artefacts.

Even the swords and helmets decorating the walls of the entrance hall are fakes, made of painted ceramic and wood, though they have acquired respectability and value as antique works of art – made in 1805 for the entrance to Cholmondelay Castle, in Cheshire, from where they are on loan.

Visitors arriving at the entrance hall with their admission ticket are offered the use of a personal tape player and earphones, for a do-it-yourself guided tour. The tape is designed for the art buff who has 45 minutes to spare, and is somewhat long for those in search of the house behind the paintings.

Look for subtleties, like the crossed foxes coat of arms of the Williamses of yore, but with the date 1988 and half-hidden signature of Christopher Boulter, painted on the walls of Watts' Hall of Fame. That tells us the mellowed William Morris-style wall covering is a modern mural, prompting closer inspection of the rest of the house.

The hall's fame is derived from portraits bequeathed to the nation by George Frederick Watts (1817-1904). who rather than wait for commissions sought sittings of those of his contemporaries he regarded as famous. His pictures include his young bride, actress Ellen Terry (1847-1928), ironically displayed above a sofa by E.W. Godwin (1833-86) – part of the furniture loaned by the Victoria and Albert Museum. Ellen Terry was Godwin's mistress. She was also the woman for whom Lewis Carroll appears to have had a deep infatuation after meeting her in 1864, when she was already married.

Like the rest of the interior, the Billiard Room is a modern presumption, created because of the solid floor – even the Victorian plaster frieze dates only from 1989. The elegant dining room contains two authentic items: a plaque inserted into the wall to display the date 1858, and the marble fireplace carved to show the Williamses watching the removal of the original block from the quarries at Carrara. Next comes the library, but don't try reaching for a book in the superb 1989 *trompe l'oeil* of Christopher Butler! The Sculpture Gallery is devoted largely to the work of the prolific John Gibson, who was born at Fforddlas in Dyffryn Conwy in 1790, and died aged 76 in Rome, where he lived for 48 years – and where his house still stands (though unmarked) in a narrow but handsome street off the Corso.

(AUGUST 1991)

BODNANT

Arboreal wonderland

BODNANT Garden, a haven of tranquillity in the Conwy Valley, caused the biggest-ever sea rescue off the North Wales coast, in 1968. Lifeboat record boards at Llandudno, Rhyl and Beaumaris all list four hundred and twenty people saved off the Little Orme after a transatlantic day out at Bodnant. They were on the 314-ton tender *St. Trillo*, drifting with a fouled propeller, after leaving Llandudno pier to return the passengers to the Swedish-American Line's 26,677 luxury ship *Kungsholm*, anchored in the bay. The *Kungsholm* was later renamed *Sea Princess*, and is now the P&O liner *Victoria*.

Liners no longer sail to Llandudno but Americans still cross the Atlantic to visit Bodnant. Yet there are people living within an hour's ride who have never explored the fragrant mysteries of Lord Aberconway's arboreal wonderland – now in the care of the National Trust.

The present baron's great-grandfather, Henry Pochin, made a fortune with a china clay mine. He bought the 1792 house in 1874 and enlarged and refaced it, his descendants adding the 18th century chimney-pieces from somewhere else. Architectural historians have never been very kind about the end result, which strangers may view from the surrounding garden, but it is the garden they have paid to see, and not the house. The house is, in any event, still the lived-in home of the Aberconway family, and is not open to the public.

Near the house, stout wooden frames support repaired branches of a twisted old tree labelled *Cedrus Atlantica Glauca*, 1876. The date tells us this was one of Henry Pochin's first judicious plantings of the big conifers that are still an interesting feature of the garden. A decade later he made similar plantings on the opposite bank of the gentle Afon Hiraethlyn, which divides the park land through a steeply sloping dell, via a dam that feeds a mill race as well as cascading the surplus water back into the original water course.

Inheriting this basic layout in 1895, Pochin's daughter, Laura McLaren, began designing the beautiful garden we know today encouraged by her politician husband Charles, who became the first Baron Aberconway in 1911. In 1901 she entrusted her plan to her eldest son Henry, who devoted half-a-century to the project, creating the magnificent terraces through which we may now wander – after paying our money at the gate.

One of the garden's most photographed features is the Pin Mill, originally a shooting lodge built in Gloucestershire in 1730, and re-erected on its present location in 1939. In a more robust way the estate's own old water mill, down in the dell, is equally attractive – from afar. Closer inspection is disappointing for it is locked, perhaps used as a garden store when it could be earning its keep as a tea shop, for all the intrepid explorers it has lured into the hollow. At this point the faint-hearted can choose between two escape routes, one encouragingly marked 'easy way up'.

Pochin's mausoleum is a feature of interest, but so, too, is the simple pet cemetery containing such marker stones as 'Mr Kipps of Bodnant, cat to the McLarens, 1943-50'.

(JUNE 1991)

BRYN EURYN

Regal ruins

NOW completely surrounded by the numerous communities that make up Colwyn Bay, the much-neglected Bryn Euryn is a forgotten gem of Welsh history, the home of Ednyfed Fychan from whom descended the House of Tudor.

The start of the main footpath leading to the summit is marked by a recently vandalised plaque in the bushes, west of the traffic lights near the junction of Rhos Road and Brompton Avenue. Another path, less easy to find, starts in Dinerth Road. Skirting an old quarry – once served by a railway running down Rhos Road to the sea – the bramble-strewn main path soon leads to the impressive ruins of an ancient two-storey fortified house, standing in splendid contrast to the rest of a town born out of the last century. This is Llys Euryn still with its massive stone fireplace and lofty chimney, and the remains of four upper storey guarderobes – medieval lavatories discharging outside the walls. Some of these ruins must have formed part of the home of Ednyfed Fychan, prime minister of Llywelyn ap Iorwerth, Prince of Wales, from about 1215.

In his youth, Ednyfed Fychan was reputed to have taken part in the Third Crusade. By 1210 he was commander of Llywelyn's army and distinguished himself against the invading army of King John of England, earning a new coat of arms of three severed Saxon heads. Still used by countless descendants all over Wales, the grisly armorial symbols were later attributed to his crusading days and became Saracen heads, for those seeking English promotion.

However it was as foreign secretary to Llywelyn Fawr (until 1240) and also to his successor, Dafydd ap Llywelyn, until they both died in 1246, that Ednyfed made most impact, turning up at such diplomatic missions as the signing of the 1218 Treaty of Worcester with Henry III.

He was buried at the nearby Llandrillo church and his eighth direct male descendant became King Henry VII, fulfilling the ancient prophecy that a Welshman would sit on the English throne. Henry imposed a permanent visual reminder of his Welsh roots on his English subjects by incorporating the Red Dragon as supporters for his redesigned Royal Arms – a feature that lasted throughout the Tudor period.

A constant stream of the good and the great, of church and state, had visited Llys Euryn, seeking Ednyfed's advice or favours, but the historic house was burnt down in 1409, during the Glyndŵr rebellion. One can only conjecture how much of the original was incorporated in its replacement, half-a-century later, by Robin ap Gruffudd Goch, whose son Huw took the surname Conway.

The Conways owned the house until 1630, and some maiden

ladies of the family continued living there as tenants. A sketch made in 1763 showed the house with three gables but by that time it was probably empty and derelict. Victorian quarrymen appear to have used it as a gunpowder store.

On the way to the magnificent views from the top of the 429ft (131m) high hill, one can see the foundations of huts put up during World War Two, for an RAF radar unit seeking out German bombers using the backdoor to Liverpool, from the captured airports of Brittany. It was for the benefit of the RAF that the wooden handrail to the summit was first erected, to help the airmen find their way at night, when all lights were prohibited. Little is known about the unit except that one airman shot and killed himself, playing Russian roulette.

It was also on the summit of Bryn Euryn that Colwyn Bay's first inhabitants built their fortified camp, and that was a long time before the arrival of the Romans.

(AUGUST 1992)

BRYN-Y-MAEN

Cathedral in the hills

BRYN-Y-MAEN, still a quiet rural backwater though part of the borough of Colwyn Bay from 1934, was the magnanimous creation of a woman born into poverty at a lonely cottage half-a-mile away. Little now remains of Rhwng-y-ddwyffordd in which Eleanor Jones was born in 1826. She was the seventh daughter of a couple who earned their daily bread bartering candles, made from rushes that the children collected. But the children's education was not neglected, for they walked five miles a day (8km) to and from Llansanffraid Glan Conwy, to attend Bryn Rhys School – which was founded by my own poor ancestors after they had drained the duck pond. This was the only site offered when they petitioned the squire of Bryn Eisteddfod estate for land for a school.

At 12 years of age Eleanor became a servant at the home of industrialist John Frost, whose wife set about re-educating her. In 1863 Eleanor, then 37, married the heir, Charles Frost, 32, and by 1874 they were living at Min-y-don Hall, Old Colwyn, the impressive former home of Richard Butler Clough. They travelled widely, including a pilgrimage to Palestine from where they returned with enough Jordan water to re-baptise all their young relatives.

When Charles Frost died in 1896, leaving everything to his widow, Eleanor inherited the extensive Bryn-y-maen farmland which overlooked her birthplace, and on which she decided to build a memorial church as the centre for a new community. She engaged famous Chester architect John Douglas to design what we should now be calling Christ Church – instead of its better-known sobriquet 'Cathedral in the hills'. Douglas also designed the Vicarage, across the road, and a house for the widowed Mrs Frost, which she called Bryn Eglwys.

Her beautiful church interior is unusual in being bereft of memorial inscriptions, though a discreet plaque, some 4 x 3 inches, has crept into the porch to record a 1983 legacy. Only at the rear of the church, beneath the east window, does one find the modest inscription: 'Built to the honour and glory of God and to the memory of Charles Frost, by Eleanor his widow. May 4th AD 1897.' This was the date the foundation stone was laid by Eleanor, whose church opened two years later, when she moved into Bryn Eglwys. The house still bears her initials and date over the doorway.

Eleanor died in 1902, and lies buried beside her husband in a fenced off grave behind the church – her details being barely readable on the granite memorial. As she left a maintenance bequest for her church one wonders whether the present-day beneficiaries have ever thought of expressing a century of gratitude by restoring her inscription?

Hoping to see Bryn-y-maen develop into a thriving community, Eleanor Frost also provided a church hall. Those responsible for extending it in 1935 added a plaque to make sure we remembered their names also!

(SEPTEMBER 1991)

CAERGWRLE

An unlikely spa

CAERGWRLE is much more than a bend in the road, once one has escaped from its narrow High Street, which forms part of the busy Mold-Wrexham road – from which drivers can risk no more than a glance at the medieval castle atop the hill ahead of them.

Dafydd ap Gruffudd turned against his brother Llywelyn in the Anglo-Welsh war of 1277. He built the castle for Edward I, who gave him 100 marks (nearly £72) to pay for the work.

Five years later Dafydd went forth from Caergwrle to attack the English in their castles at Fflint. Hawarden and Rhuddlan, thus starting the 1282 war in which his brother was killed, he was executed, and Wales was annexed to England.

Edward rebuilt the war-damaged castle in 1282 and gave it to Queen Eleanor in 1284. It passed through various hands until 1961, when the Earl of Derby gave it to the parish council – a gift recorded on a plaque on the bend in the road.

The plaque marks the start of a steep and poorly maintained path, to the top of the lofty outcrop of top-quality millstone grit on which the impressive remains of the castle still stand. A signpost to the path was erected to meet a deficiency noted when this feature first appeared in the *Daily Post*.

Beside the start of the path is the war memorial, bearing the names of sixty local men, including three awarded the MM, who were killed in World War One, and another thirty-six in World War Two. They included Captain C.C. Trevor-Roper and Private G. Trevor-Roper from 1914-18, and Flight-Lieutenant R.D. Trevor-Roper, DFC, DFM, from 1939-45, reminding us of

37

the family who lived until recently at Plas Teg, the three-storeyed house with a square tower at each corner, which Sir John Trevor built in 1610 on the northern approaches. Sir John was elected MP for Denbighshire in 1620, and of Flintshire in 1624 and 1625. He died in 1673.

Beyond the war memorial is the former magistrates' court, police station and local gaol, still with barred windows. It was replaced in 1970 by the present police station on the opposite side of the road. A walk down Castle Street takes one to the heart of old Caergwrle: the fork to the left leading to a picturesque but half-forgotten packhorse bridge over Afon Alun, while that to the right leads to the more obvious 1838 road-bridge to Hope. This is well worth closer examination for it crosses a weir that has been colonised by several varieties of duck. It used to serve the sluice, still in situ, of an undershot wheel at the mill, now converted into a smart house.

A private drive just beyond the mill leads to Rhyddan Hall, now the worse for wear but built in 1749 by the Glynns, made famous by proxy when W.E. Gladstone married into the family. A short distance up the drive a derelict Ruabon brick building still bears the inscription Caergwrle Natural Waters, a reminder of the village's very brief fame as a spa, early in the last century, when the railway station used to be listed as 'Caergwrle Castle and Wells'.

Caergwrle was simultaneously more famous for its ale, but the old brewery was demolished in 1991. The village still has a surfeit of pubs, built not to sell Caergwrle Ale to the locals but to refresh the hundreds of Edwardian railway passengers who once sought the Wells and their promise of improved health.

(NOVEMBER 1991)

CAERNARFON

Rome's Segontium

SEGONTIUM revisited brought back all the exhilaration of my childhood introduction to this half-forgotten outpost of the Roman Empire. The 2nd Adiutrix Legion built Segontium in 78 AD, and were soon followed by the 20th Legion, who remained in occupation until AD 390. Caernarfon's Romans left an indelible impression on the Welsh folk memory, including the tradition, first recorded in the ninth century, that Constantine, son of an Emperor, was buried here.

In 1283, when building St Mary's church within his fortified town of Caernarfon, Edward I reburied the remains of an august warrior named Constantine, found under an inscribed stone. There is some confusion as to whether Edward thought he had found the son of Constantine the Great, or Constantine's father, Constantius, Emperor in the West (whom we now know died at York), or even the son of Magnus Maximus. The Constantinian influence on Edward was such that he fashioned Caernarfon castle on what he had seen at Constantinople during the Crusades, complete with multifaceted towers and horizontal decorative bands in the outer stonework. One could still be mistaken for the other.

By about 1300 the famous Dream of Macsen Wledig, in the *Mabinogion*, told of the romance which blossomed at Segontium between the Roman emperor Magnus Maximus and the Welsh princess Helen – later confused with the Empress St Helen, mother of Constantine the Great. Thus the folk memory has given Caernarfon street names like St Helen's Road and Constantine Terrace, and a rock-solid belief that at least one of the Constantines served at Segontium, guardian of the Roman mineral wealth of North Wales.

More by accident than design, much of the fort's outer wall and three of its gates have survived, enclosing an area twice as big as Caernarfon's better known medieval castle, half-a-mile away. Yet only a handful of the tourists who flock from the four corners of the world to see Edward's castle ever make that extra half-mile (800m) journey to Segontium.

Segontium is the Cinderella of the National Museum of Wales, and there is not so much as a guidebook on sale to interpret this gem – the only Roman fort in Wales where the foundations of the original buildings are exposed. Its buildings were rediscovered in 1845, when a new vicarage was being built beside the Beddgelert road – which perpetuates the Roman road from the east gate. In 1913 developers turned their attention to the opposite side of the road and actually built a couple of houses before the Cambrian Archaeological Association was able to buy up the rest of the fort.

Today's visitors can walk the Roman streets, explore the surviving gates, walk down stone steps into the strong room of the Roman HQ, examine the commandant's heated bath-house, and generally transport themselves back in time. In the tiny, and wholly inadequate museum, built by the National Trust in 1937, one may see the altars at which Romans worshipped, until Constantine's conversion to Christianity in 312. One of these was found as recently as 1959, in the well-preserved remains of a slate-roofed Mithraic lodge, at a site outside the fort that is now marked by a plaque on the wall of 16 Lon-y-bryn.

Mithraism was a kind of Roman freemasonry, open only to men, via seven degrees of ritual initiation, each designed to take them into ever closer communion with their Sun-god, who offered protection from the forces of evil. The Caernarfon Mithraeum was the only one found in Wales, and appears to have been abandoned in 293 when its Rhineland builders, the 1st Cohort of Sunici, of the 20th Legion, were replaced by another regiment. The name of the Sunici is preserved on a 3rd century slate plaque in the museum, telling us the fort's aqueduct 'which had collapsed through age' (thought to be a face-saving euphemism for 'destroyed by the natives'), was

40

restored by the regiment under the Imperial Caesars Septimus Severus, Marcus Antoninus (known as Caracalla) and Geta, i.e. shortly before 211 AD, when Caracalla ordered the assassination of Geta.

(NOVEMBER 1991)

CAERNARFON

The airport

CAERNARFON Airport was opened in 1975, but had an earlier existence as RAF Llandwrog, built to defend Liverpool against German attack from captured French airfields in Brittany. It has recently been upgraded, notably with the installation of runway lighting, which would enable it to operate regular services to Cardiff, but its main use is as a popular centre for short pleasure flights and a thriving flying club, where many North Wales residents have qualified as pilots.

In 1940 it was known simply as 'the rabbit warren', when the 46th (Liverpool Welsh) Royal Tank Regiment earmarked nearby Glynllifon park for training. Trying to save his magnificent gardens from mutilation, Lord Newborough offered his Warren as an alternative. The Army land agent, at 28 Station Road, Colwyn Bay, replied: 'The ground, being sandy, will not be suitable for tank manoeuvres,' little knowing that the regiment's first action would be in the deserts of Egypt!

When the French surrender gave the Luftwaffe a backdoor to Britain in 1940, the Air Ministry requisitioned the Warren for the construction of a fighter aerodrome, but it was no longer needed by Fighter Command when completed in 1941. Its first aircraft was a Lysander, which made a forced landing on March 25, having flown from RAF Ringway, today better known as Manchester International Airport. Its first of many fatal accidents was in June 1941, when an Oxford crashed into the sea on take-off. Four months later I was a chorister at the funeral service, in Caernarfon, for seventeen airmen killed when a descending Whitley bomber landed on the back of another as it was taking off. All seventeen coffins were taken to Llanbeblig church on an aircraft low-loader transporter (known as a Queen Mary), and some were buried in the local cemetery, but most were taken to the railway station for dispersal.

In 1979 I was privileged to write the first short history of the aerodrome, noting such incidents as the only enemy attack, in January 1942, when a lone Junkers 88 machine-gunned the station, damaging one Whitley bomber used for air-gunnery training. The aerodrome's revenge was spectacular, contributing three of its training Whitleys and six of its instructors for the world's first 1,000 bomber raid, on Cologne, in May 1942. Two of the instructors were killed when their aircraft was shot down on the way home: Sergeant W.H. Orman, wounded and trapped in the rear gun turret, and Pilot Officer Dennis Box, thrown out of the disintegrating aircraft before he had time to attach his observer-type parachute to his two chest hooks. Seconds before the disintegration Box passed a parachute to the skipper, Squadron-Leader John Russell, who managed to clip it on while falling through space, and survived.

The high rate of accidents among wartime trainees, pushing weary aircraft to their limits, led to the formation at Llandwrog of the first RAF mountain rescue team, at the instigation of the station medical officer, Flight-Lieutenant G.W. Graham, whose traditions are now maintained at RAF Valley.

RAF flying ended in June 1945, after which the aerodrome was used until 1956 to store and disarm vast quantities of high explosive and deteriorating gas bombs, the latter being dipped in concrete (ostensibly to seal them!) before being despatched by sea for dumping in Beaufort's Dyke, between Scotland and Northern Ireland, and another location to the north of the Irish Republic. Beaufort's Dyke was used for a similar purpose after the 1914-18 War. The airfield was used briefly in 1969 to accommodate the two thousand troops who took part in the

Investiture of Prince Charles at Caernarfon Castle.

Something of its wartime story is told in a surprisingly good museum, open to visitors – as is the original RAF control tower, now converted into a cafe.

(JUNE 1994)

CAERNARFON

Majestic demise

BANGOR Street, once Caernarfon's cultural and political centre, is a sorry sight since the fire that destroyed the Majestic Fun Pub at the beginning of 1994. The site is now an open space beside the recently refurbished Celtic Royal Hotel.

A short street, it starts at the Majestic and ends in Turf Square, which was once the venue for the oat market, the pillory and the stocks. In the 17th century it was known as Llanfair Street, because Caernarfon's citizens were largely unaware of life east of Llanfair-is-gaer, now known as Y Felinheli. Later it was called Boot Street, when Caernarfon thoughts ended at the Boot Inn which stood in the middle of the road at the western end. The street still has two pubs, the Prince of Wales, opposite the Majestic site, and the Ship and Castle at the other end (the street's oldest surviving building).

Some of us can remember when the nearby corner shop facing the Square, now occupied by an insurance broker, was adorned with a gilded crown and the words 'Purveyors of medicines to Queen Victoria'. Pompous officials preparing for the present Queen's first visit to Caernarfon, in 1953, descended upon the old pharmacy and forced the removal of this historic and ornate Victorian claim for which no Royal Warrant had ever been sought (and which, in any case, would have expired). The claim was, in fact, quite accurate for, five years before her 1837 Coronation, Princess Victoria and her mother were guests of the Marquess of Anglesey at Plas Newydd. When the princess took ill the Marquess sent his yacht across the Menai Strait to buy a remedy at Caernarfon. The old pharmacy's final blow came soon after 1953 when the elderly proprietor retired after routine test prescriptions by the new NHS inspectors revealed worrying discrepancies which were quickly traced to one and a half centuries of energetic polishing of the delicate brass weighing equipment.

Standing markedly taller than all the other buildings is one emblazoned 'Liberal Club'. Once the headquarters of Lloyd George during his fifty-five years as local MP, it is now a snooker club, although the Liberal Democrats retain ownership and use of a tiny committee room. It is badly in need of a liberal coat of paint.

Across the road is Pendref Independent Chapel, bearing the confusing date of 1791. The town's oldest Nonconformist cause was founded on this site in 1782 in a building replaced in 1791, 1819 and again in 1838, enlarged in 1862 and given its present appearance in 1881.

The Majestic, which was converted into a drinking club in the early 1980s, was built as a one thousand and fifty seat cinema, and opened on 11 August 1934 with the screening of *Evergreen*, starring Jessie Mathews and Sonja Hale. During the war the seating was reduced to eight hundred to enable the stage to be extended for some memorable ENSA concerts, intended mainly for the many servicemen camped in the area. This was the stage on which local soprano Anne Edwards made her name in two memorable concerts during the cinema's 20th anniversary year, before moving on to the Carl Rosa Opera, the Welsh National Opera, Sadler's Wells and such exotic venues as Hong Kong and the Shah of Persia's royal opening of the Teheran Opera House (Rudaki Hall), where she was the principal soprano in *Nabucco* – a strange choice for a Muslim state (albeit one with thirty synagogues). The Shah was deposed by Shiite Muslim fundamentalists two years later.

Across the road was where I made my only foray into the world of singing, as a boy soprano in the then famous paid choir (£2.62 a year) of the impressively full Christ Church, which opened in 1864 for the town's monoglot Anglicans. A century later it lost its congregation because of diminishing worship and growing affinity for the Welsh language, and had been derelict for several decades before reopening in 2000 as a children's fun centre, which has preserved the outer architecture and retained a few of the interior features.

At the opposite end of the street the Institute, bearing the misleading date of 1884, still houses the Royal Town Council. But it has lost much of the glory with which it opened in 1886, to provide public bathrooms, a library, meeting rooms, and an art studio where a well-known local lady posed nude in 1953.

(JANUARY 1994)

CAERNARFON

Castle Square

CAERNARFON's Castle Square, once the jewel in the crown of the Welsh tourist industry, is now but a grey shadow of its glorious past, in a town which seemed to give up the will to live after losing its fight to become the capital of Wales in 1955.

There is little hope of regeneration in the Square, to match what is beginning to happen in the heartland of the old town, until something is done about the deep overgrown scar on the abandoned site of Swyddfa'r Herald, destroyed by fire in 1984. This was the ugly, ill-equipped, but powerful office of the old-style *Caernarvon & Denbigh Herald*, where I once laboured to record the town's struggle for official recognition, editing the paper during 1953.

History was on its side, with many old reference books listing Caernarfon as the Welsh capital. Caernarfon was purpose-built as the vice-regal outpost of Edward I, designed to control Wales. The Romans had the same idea a thousand years earlier, when they made Caernarfon their western outpost of the Legionary HQ at Chester.

Upstart Cardiff outmanoeuvred the old town in 1955, and Caernarfon had to make do with a consolation prize eight years later, when the Queen told an enormous crowd in Castle Square that she wished to single them out for a special privilege, adding in Welsh: 'Felly penodaf Gaernarfon i fod yn Fwrdeisdref Frenhinol' (*Therefore I declare Caernarfon to be a Royal Borough*).

Alas the town was already in decay and the honour had turned politically sour by 1969, when the Queen next looked down on Castle Square from Queen Eleanor's gate to present Prince Charles to the people after his Investiture.

Beneath Eleanor's gate is Sir Goscombe John's famous bronze statue of local MP David Lloyd George, shaking his fist, as though in despair at the impoverished shops before him. This was the once-mighty commercial hub of what many will remember as Caernarfonshire's principal market town.

In the middle of the Square, or Y Maes, as it is usually known among the citizens, there is another bronze statue: of Sir Hugh Owen (1804-1881), described as a tireless philanthropist who devoted his life to the furtherance of non-sectarian education at every level.

The Post Office displays a 1953 bronze plaque to remind us of the pioneering radio experiments of local man Sir William Preece, who gave the unknown young Marconi his first job in Britain. It was from behind the Royal Arms on the roof of the Post Office that a radio-equipped director of music stood during the 1969 Investiture, baton in hand, to conduct royal trumpeters playing fanfares from the battlements of the Castle, on the opposite side of the Square.

Still bearing its date, 1883, the historic old People's Cafe is now called Cadora. Closed in 1995, the former Bertorelli's ice-cream shop and cafe was probably the last place to have its old gas lamps in situ when it shut, after some 75 years as a family-run business.

Whatever its deficiencies in the 21st century, Caernarfon is a fascinating old town, and an essential element in the educational process of anyone trying to plumb the depths of Welsh history and politics.

(NOVEMBER 1992)

CAERNARFON

Palace Street

CAERNARFON's Palace Street, which retains the dimensions and grid pattern of the medieval town built by Edward I, was pedestrianised in 1993, in a process which briefly revealed some of its ancient underground mysteries.

Having written the history of Palace Street more than 40 years earlier I rewalked the one Caernarfon street with hopes for a commercial future and tourist boost, in the otherwise depressed and scruffy former heartland of north Wales.

The street takes its name from Plas Puleston, home of Richard de Puleston, who was appointed sheriff of Caernarvonshire in 1284, and his father Roger, who was appointed tax collector for Wales in 1293. That was the year of the rebellion led by Madog, nephew of Llywelyn ap Gruffudd, who captured the unfinished castle and turned on the Anglo-Norman bureaucrats, hanging Roger the taxman from the upper storey of his own home.

If the first English Prince of Wales really was born at Caernarfon in 1284 it would have been at Plas Puleston, when the castle we know today was little more than a building site. However, the prince was probably born at Rhuddlan Castle.

Plas Puleston was on the site now stretching from the

solicitors' office at No.2 to the glass and china shop known as Leeds House – famous in my youth as an ice cream and coffee stop. Here young people would gather for hours of harmless debate. Having given the street its original name, this interesting block of buildings also gave it the name of Red Lion Street for much of the 19th century.

When I wrote my history of the street, No.2 was the thriving tripe shop of Mr and Mrs J. Twyerould – they sold nothing else, but lived very well on it, in the economic pattern of independent shopkeepers on which Caernarfon used to thrive, in those hard-working days of minuscule incomes, before the advent of the universal motor car and the omnipresent supermarket. Mr Twyerould told me there was a red lion carving on either side of the door when he took over the premises in 1937. This used to be the Red Lion Vaults, although the name was changed in 1903 to Palace Hotel, a grand title for a tiny establishment which was stripped of its licence in 1910. Next door, at No 4, stood the Red Lion Tavern, which lost its licence in 1905.

A century ago Palace Street housed ten pubs, and there were another 59 in the rest of the little town! I remember just two: the Newborough Arms, now an attractive house called Llys Llywelyn, dated 1776, and The Vaults, now a shop called the 14th Peak. A new pub has materialised under the name of Y Goron Fach, which I remember as one of the street's several butchers' shops, although before that it was the Victoria Vaults. The biggest building in the street is the old Market Hall, whose once informative slate plaque is in need of a good scrub, so that we might once again know it was built in 1832. It marks the site of Plas Mawr, a Tudor mansion which looked very similar to its namesake in Conwy. It was a refuge for paupers by 1809 but part of it was a famous school until 1831. Its cellars remained in use until very recently as a Customs & Excise bonded warehouse.

The 1993 roadworks revealed that the carriageway had been

resting on a network of vaulted cellars and tunnels, which having safely carried the heavy traffic of several hundred years had to be filled with concrete for the pedestrianisation process!

(OCTOBER 1993)

CAERNARFON

Tros yr Aber

TROS YR ABER is not a name you will find on any map or road sign. It means 'across the river mouth' and has been used for countless centuries to describe the left bank of Afon Seiont, where it spills out into the Menai Strait through a 50 yard (45m) gap at Caernarfon.

Pedestrian access is simple, via a swing bridge by the Eagle Tower of Caernarfon Castle. Vehicle access is restricted to those familiar with the complex lanes some distance away, off the Porthmadog road.

The first swing bridge of 1900 (a date that gave it its name, Ladysmith Bridge), was designed to carry cars and other light vehicles. It was demolished in the mid-1960s, and apart from a temporary Bailey bridge for the Investiture of Prince Charles in 1969, was not replaced until the present pedestrian bridge was opened in 1973.

There was an amusing incident during the period when the river mouth was without a bridge, when Lord Snowdon and I agreed to meet at Tros yr Aber in 1968. As Constable of Caernarfon Castle (and then husband of Princess Margaret) he was planning the artistic side of the following year's Investiture spectacular. There is no better place from which to view the castle than Tros yr Aber, and as we knew each other, and each of us was familiar from childhood with the complex alternative route, we agreed to meet on the other side of the river for an exclusive *Daily Post* photograph, leaving the Fleet Street horde running up and down the opposite quayside, trying to hire boats.

Retracing my steps in 1993, I called in at the 103-acre Coed Helen estate – recognisable by the 1891 top lodge inscribed with the interesting play on words *Oriens Morior Moriens Orior* (meaning something like 'The rising sun dies, Moriens is born'). Bought by Caernarfon Borough Council during 1950-51, the estate is now leased to two caravan operators, with the old house used for offices and a shop, but still retaining a carved stone dated 1605 and bearing the initials of Sir William Thomas and his wife Gaynor.

Coed Helen is generally accepted as the correct name, derived either from Princess Helen of the *Mabinogion* or the Empress Helen, mother of Constantine the Great, but the people of Caernarfon always describe it as Coed Alun, and it was written as *Koedalen* at least as early as 1605.

Caravanners now use the family's once very private footpath down to the crenellated bottom lodge, which is used as a watchroom by the bridgekeeper. Around the little headland I was glad to see that the primitive open air swimming pool, an eyesore for the best part of a century, had been removed. It was Caernarfon's only contribution to the Victorian dream of joining the newfangled seaside resorts like Llandudno, Colwyn Bay and Rhyl, sprouting along the coast in the wake of the railway.

A little further on the old Caernarfon Golf Club has blossomed into an 18-hole course with a posh new club house and bar which is about as far as Caernarfon people travel along this road. Beyond it, in a walled enclosure in the middle of a field, is the very interesting church of St. Baglan, mostly medieval but still used for occasional services, despite a plaque in the porch saying the Church in Wales gave it away in 1991 to the Friends of Friendless Churches. Among the interesting tombstones is one for the ashes of Princess Margaret's father-in-law, Ronald Armstrong-Jones, QC, of nearby Plas Dinas, who died in 1966 and was cremated at Colwyn Bay.

(JULY 1993)

CAERWYS

Home of the Eisteddfod

CAERWYS, now promoting itself as the smallest town in Great Britain, was once proud to be known as the biggest town in Flintshire, and home of the county assizes. Until 1672 this was where the circuit judge would sit three times a year, to try all cases of serious crime in the county that Edward I had created as an annexe to his Earldom of Chester.

Whether one now sees Caerwys as a small town or a big village, it oozes civic pride in its history, even though it was a year late in celebrating the 400th anniversary of its most famous event: the Caerwys eisteddfod of 1567. Unabashed, the people simply refused to bow to all the scholars who told them, with overwhelming evidence, that their 1968 celebrations were based on a misunderstanding of old calendars, combined with a 400-year-old clerical error. The celebrations went ahead and countless souvenirs were produced, including the costly registration of an official coat of arms to replace the spurious design devised by a local artist at the beginning of the century for a travelling Bohemian pottery salesman. (My father was similarly inventive in providing the Bohemians with a coat of arms for Garndolbenmaen).

Caerwys was more accurate in 1990 with its celebrations for the 700th anniversary of its charter, granted by Edward I to create a borough unique among the ten new English colonies in north Wales, in that it allowed the admission of Welshmen as freemen. Princess Margaret, Countess of Snowdon, visited Caerwys for the 1990 celebrations, an event now commemorated in a plaque on a circle of raised stones known in folk memory as The Cross, presumably once the site of the market cross, in the centre of the town's original medieval grid pattern. Another less likely suggestion is that it was once the site of a cross used as a resting place by burial parties carrying coffins to the parish church. The old cross has long since disappeared and today a tree grows in its place. A second plaque tells us it was planted as part of the 1968 celebrations, by the Earl of Plymouth, Lord of the Manor of Caerwys. The present tree replaces one planted in 1919 to mark the end of the Great War, which replaced an even earlier tree.

As part of the 1990 celebrations the little town's more interesting buildings were identified with illustrated boards telling something of their history. Unfortunately they were not made weatherproof and some are difficult to read. It was a highly commendable civic exercise and one wonders whether it could be repeated with more permanent boards, seeing that Caerwys has so much to reveal to the visitor.

In practice Caerwys does not have many visitors, although it is well worth a detour. Though very near the A55 road, Caerwys is somewhat isolated, a factor which resulted in the loss of its market. At the turn of the century there were eight public houses for the refreshment of travellers. There are still three.

Turn down any street to see interesting old houses, some displaying their former use in such names as Peniel Chapel, Old Jail or Old Court. Bell House, at the town centre, reminds us this was the place where the market bell used to be rung.

(MARCH 1994)

CAPEL CURIG

Queen Victoria's graffiti

CAPEL CURIG is a straggling thinly-populated community, clinging to one of the narrowest and most tortuous sections of

Thomas Telford's London-Holyhead road. Despite its school, church, inns and shops, Capel Curig never quite blossomed into a cohesive village. Were we still travelling by horse we would see it as an attractive place, but modern traffic conditions make it almost impossible to stop.

On leaving Betws-y-coed one is confronted by Tŷ Hyll which, like everything that is best in Capel Curig, is situated on an acute bend. Now the headquarters and information centre of the Snowdonia National Park Society, Tŷ Hyll has about half-a-dozen parking spaces. It does not deserve its name, which means Ugly House. On the contrary it is exceedingly picturesque, having been meticulously built with some enormous natural stones calculated to weigh up to three tons. Its origins are lost in history but local tradition says it was built in 1475 by two outlaw brothers.

Tŷ Hyll remained remote until Telford abandoned the original turnpike road, which was susceptible to flooding, and built a bridge in 1819 to bring his A5 past the front door. Recently refurbished inside, and furnished by the Welsh National Folk Museum, Tŷ Hyll now looks like an early 19th century cottage.

The next object to catch the traveller's eye is the stage coach outside Ty'n-y-coed Hotel. It looks authentic but is really a recent replica of the original 19th century vehicle, which turned up at Capel Curig after its use in the 1939 filming of Daphne du Maurier's novel *Jamaica Inn*.

Now permanently removed for restoration and preservation, the original stage coach found its way to Wales via actor and playwright Emlyn Williams, who starred in the film with Charles Laughton, Maureen O'Hara and Robert Newton.

Another colourful inn at Capel Curig is Cobden's. It takes its name not from the Victorian politician Richard Cobden, as is commonly assumed (because of his friendship with John Bright, who loved these parts) but from a once famous cricketer. Frank

Carroll Cobden was 83 when he died here in 1932, his being the first English family to settle in Capel Curig. He made his name in 1870 when, as captain of the Cambridge XI, he took three Oxford wickets with three balls – and eight wickets for 76 runs. The ball, suitably inscribed, was auctioned at Christie's in about 1990-91.

For many years Capel Curig's most famous hostelry was the Royal Hotel, built in 1804 on the original turnpike road. Its window panes bore the diamond-inscribed signatures of Princess (later Queen) Victoria, Byron and Walter Scott. Bypassed by Telford's A5 road, the Royal is now Plas y Brenin National Mountain Centre.

The parish church, built in 1883, was closed at the beginning of 1992, and is never likely to reopen.

(JULY 1992)

CARMEL

Looking to Constantinople

A MONASTERY of the Greek Orthodox faith is the last thing one expects to find in the Welsh-speaking Nonconformist village of Carmel, on the bleak north-western slopes of Mynydd Cilgwyn.

Spotting the heraldic eagle of St. John on a chapel gatepost, I read at its feet a plaque telling me I had arrived at Mynachdy Sant Ioan Fedyddiwr (that is Welsh for Monastery of St John the Baptist). An English notice explains it is part of the American Orthodox Catholic Patriarchate Inc, and the gates are adorned with the distinctive Greek cross, but the inscription on the facade of the chapel is 'Pisgah 1861'.

A hundred yards up the hill sits a bigger chapel of the same name, belonging to the Welsh Independents, and bearing the date 1877. The village also has Carmel chapel, built in 1871 by the Calvinistic Methodists (to give the community its present name), but a fourth chapel, also built by the Calvinists, was converted into a house some years ago. The Anglican church never established itself here.

The chapels tell most of the story of a God-fearing community which grew out of the 18th century reopening of the Mynydd Cilgwyn slate quarries, first used by the Romans or maybe earlier. 'We are in the Welsh Holy Land, surrounded by villages bearing the Biblical names of Carmel, Nazareth, Caesarea, Nebo, Golan, Bethel, Bethesda,' said Cheshire-born Father Demetrius, who founded the Monastery with his Irish mother, Sister Anna.

Rising out of the silvery Mediterranean, the first Carmel or Kerem-El, meaning Vineyard of the Lord, is dominated by Stella Maris monastery (Star of the Sea), where I spent a memorable year of my youth with 6th Airborne Division Signals Intelligence. Rising out of Caernarfon Bay, the other Carmel is surprisingly well served by Silver Star buses. I am familiar, too, with the original Pisgah, though under its better-known name of Nebo, in the Kingdom of Jordan, from where, like Moses before us, one can look down on the Judaean desert and across the mountains to Jerusalem, in the Promised Land.

'From my Pisgah I can look down on a daily reminder of Byzantium,' said Father Demetrius, referring to Caernarfon Castle, whose distinctive architecture replicates what Edward I saw at Constantinople, on his way home from the Crusades – and it is to Constantinople (now Istanbul), and not Athens that the Greek churches still turn for their leadership.

Father Demetrius bought the old Baptist chapel in 1991 from Ken Whatnell, who had partially converted it into a house, in which he wrote his book *Before the Bomb*, this being his own interpretation of the Bible's message. The original baptistry remains intact and has been incorporated into Carmel's Orthodox Church – the Eastern churches also practise total immersion.

'Most of the early Welsh saints were Orthodox Celts, pupils of Bretons taught at Alexandria. I am merely helping to bring back that which has been lost,' claimed Father Demetrius. But Archbishop Gregorios, of the Archdiocese of Thyateira and Great Britain, head of the Greek Orthodox Church in the UK, sent the *Daily Post* a lengthy letter distancing himself from the Welsh Carmel, and the monastery established under the aegis of the American Orthodox Catholic Patriarchate Inc.

'Neither I nor any of my predecessors have given the necessary blessing to open a Greek Orthodox monastery in that village,' said the Archbishop, but he had the good grace to send me 'many blessings'. The denial does not detract from the novelty of exploring this exotic establishment on its bleak Welsh mountain top!

(NOVEMBER 1992)

CERRIGYDRUDION

A place of stones

CERRIGYDRUDION is a community whose natives travel far but come home to die, judging from various memorials in the well-positioned church, which is centuries older than its 1981-82 restoration might suggest. Though the population is small, with five hundred electors on the register, Cerrigydrudion is a reasonably complete Welsh village of yesteryear. Bypassed many decades ago, the village still has several shops, a bank, a post office, resident rector, three chapels, three pubs, a school, a garage, a fire station and a police station.

It even has a library two days a week, in the converted 1911 home of the old one-horse parish hearse. Villagers who remember the ornate hearse in use also tell of its being retired to the neighbouring community of Pentrellyncymmer, where it was allowed to rot away. It was useless by the time a London antique dealer scoured North Wales in the early 1960s, paying

£25 a time for old parish hearses earmarked for a new lease of life in the United States as cocktail cabinets.

The National School is now the church hall and the British School a thriving snooker club. Both were replaced by the bland but useful building put up by the old Denbighshire County Council in 1971. An unusually robust stone bus shelter has a tablet telling us (in Welsh) that it commemorates the 1951 Festival of Britain. It also reminds us that the Festival of Britain was a popular success which left us with many permanent improvements throughout the land. It certainly was compared with the politically inflated non event called the Millennium!

Across the road a full inscription tells us (also in Welsh) that the six alms houses were provided in 1717 by Judge Robert Price, of Giler, which is now a farm. Although Giler is some miles away, the name appears repeatedly inside the church, where there is a separate Giler Chapel opening off the small chancel. Its oldest memorial is for Thomas Price, who died in 1667. Beside it is a memorial erected by the above 'Mr Baron Robert Price', ostensibly for his mother who died aged 89, in 1723, but also listing the achievements of her eight children. Heading the list is the selfsame Robert Price, 'Sergeant at law and one of the barons of His Majesty's court of Exchequer at Westminster'. His plaque tells us his two brothers became Freemen of London, and that his sisters married into the well-known Meyrick, Kyffin, Maysmore, Burchinshaw and Wynne families of north Wales.

Lesser mortals, like Margaret, wife of John Jones of the White Lion, who died in 1813, are also commemorated in the church. The White Lion still looks out on the square, opposite the Queen's Hotel which carries the date 1417, presumably referring to the original building. The third inn, which is outside the main community, is the Saracen's Head, beside the A5 road.

The chapels are dated: Moriah, 1876 (Independent); Jerusalem, 1899 (Presbyterian); and Seion, 1883 (Wesleyan). The remains of the much older original Sion plaque was recently rediscovered in the wall of what is now a private house.

(OCTOBER 1991)

CHIRK

Hotbed of intrigue

CHIRK CASTLE is an especially good place to visit for students of the Civil War especially, we are told, since the 1992 celebrations for the 350th anniversary of that strange epoch in English history. To emphasise the celebrations 'the King's bedroom' was opened to the public, complete with very ornate four-poster inscribed: 'King Charles I slept in this bed, September 22-28th, 1645'.

'Perhaps it would be more accurate if it said Marion Davies slept in this bed with Randolph Hearst,' suggested Lady Margaret Myddleton, a tenant of one wing of the castle and owner of all its furniture. Her late husband's family owned Chirk for four centuries but it now belongs to the National Trust, which has added the 'King's bedroom' and its state bed to what the public may see. It was her husband, Colonel Ririd Myddleton, who chanced to rediscover and retrieve the family bed which an ancestor had sent off to the sale room in Queen Victoria's time.

'King Charles certainly spent some time at Chirk during the Civil War but he never slept in that bed,' Lady Margaret told me. 'The bed came from Wanstead, in Essex, in 1761, when Lady Elizabeth Rushout married Richard Myddleton. After being sold from Chirk in the 19th century it was eventually bought by American newspaper millionaire Randolph Hearst, for his new 1925 home at St. Donat's Castle, in the Vale of Glamorgan,' added Lady Margaret.

St. Donat's was run by Hearst's resident mistress, film

actress Marion Davies. The bed was sold to the antique trade when the Hearst publishing empire collapsed in the 1930s. Hearst died in 1951, and Marion Davies a decade later. Ultimately that fully authenticated connection with the man who inspired the film *Citizen Kane* may be of greater interest than King Charles to the eighty thousand people who visit Chirk during the course of a year.

'It is the sort of bed the King would have slept in,' suggested the National Trust, although they need not have been so apologetic, for Hearst had shown the plaque to several visitors to St. Donat's, and it might also have been in place when the bed first came to Chirk over two hundred years ago.

Meanwhile visitors can enjoy the 13th century castle and 1636 modernisation which the King certainly knew. The east wing was again modernised in 1845, by Augustus Pugin, partner in the design of the Houses of Parliament. It is unusual in that it has always been lived in, its furnishings accruing through successive generations.

Taking pride of place in the Long Gallery is a Dutch ebony cabinet, decorated with silver and twelve Flemish paintings on copper. The family believes they are by Rubens. It came to Chirk on the restoration of the monarchy, a gift from Charles II to Sir Thomas Myddleton, in lieu of the peerage he had declined. Perhaps Sir Thomas was troubled by his conscience for having supported both sides in the Civil War.

(JULY 1992)

CILCAIN

A pleasant retreat

CILCAIN has suffered more from English attempts at spelling Welsh than most villages. It was listed as Chiluan in the Domesday Book of 1086, since when it has been written with many variations, including Kilken (1699) which is preserved in parish church memorials to the Kilken Hall branch of the Mostyn family.

Still pronounced Kilken by the residents, the current spelling would appear to be correct, derived from Cil (retreat) and Cain (pleasant), and that remains a perfect description for one of Wales's most attractive villages (though it is a pity about someone's habit of dumping rubbish in the otherwise neat car park).

Cilcain is quite unspoilt by the recent discreet addition to its medieval framework of many good-quality houses. The old village is a cluster of no more than a couple of dozen houses sitting astride its narrow cross-roads, whose boundaries are defined by solid stone structures dating back through the centuries.

One of the most obvious is the attractive White Horse Inn, which has a thriving dining room for the steady stream of intrepid walkers returning from their exploration of the nearby summit of Moel Famau. But beware of the notice on the front door: 'Will customers with dogs or walking boots please use the other bar. Thank you.' The 16th century White Horse is the last of Cilcain's seven inns, several of which are recognisable. Llys Eifion used to be the Red Lion, still locked into the folk memory as the scene of a nasty 18th century fight between the innkeeper and a Methodist minister who had taken to preaching outside the house. Ty'n-llan, occupying one of the corners at the cross-roads, is another old inn, remembered as the residence of the engineer during the brief era when Cilcain thought it had struck gold in the nearby hills. The Old Smithy, occupying another corner, and dating from 1572, has been converted into a smart house but retains the outside stone steps to the original loft.

Cilcain's glory however is its church, whose beautifully carved roof, one of the most impressive in Britain, is said to have been moved from Basingwerk Abbey in 1535, and restored in 1846, 1889 and 1937. All that remains of the Norman church is the carved font, now on the floor at the rear of the church, together with some 14th century stone sarcophagus lids, and an interesting collection of fourteen brass pew plates of the old families who once ruled here. The east window contains glass from 1546, while the place on the east wall often reserved for the Ten Commandments is here taken up with a memorial to nine Mostyns – much the same thing in these parts.

An unusual relic in the church is a banner saying: 'Cilcen for God and Church'. It was carried in protest processions through London in 1912, and Wrexham in 1913, during the campaign against the disestablishment from the Church of England of what became the autonomous Church in Wales in 1920.

(SEPTEMBER 1992)

CLYNNOG FAWR

An Old-Welsh bastion

CLYNNOG FAWR is one of our oldest communities, yet remains but a small hamlet, albeit with a church of massive proportions to remind us of its role on the ancient pilgrims' route to Ynys Enlli *(Bardsey)*. Clynnog is the reputed burial place of St Beuno, a seventh century holy man, although Ynys Enlli and Nefyn make rival claims, and another dozen churches are dedicated in his honour.

Beuno was living beside the Severn, in mid Wales, when he heard a Saxon on the opposite bank. 'These strange-tongued men will take this place,' predicted Beuno, and promptly led his people first to Holywell and later Clynnog, to avoid the foreign tongue and to protect old-Welsh Christianity, which far predated the Augustinian mission of 597.

At Clynnog, Beuno founded a religious order of matching importance to that surrounding the episcopal seat at Bangor, which was reflected in the rebuilding of the church in 1480. Today's chancel and transepts are of 1480, with the nave being added in 1500. The tower and St Beuno's chapel were added in the 16th century, and linked to an interesting vaulted passage in the 17th century or earlier. Interesting medieval features in the chancel include three stone seats built into the south wall, for clergy waiting to assist in the mass. Fourteen miserericorde choir stalls, suggest the original users were elderly holy men.

Some 200 yards (180m) south of the church, a roadside well bears the name of St Beuno. A gateway leads into a small walled enclosure with stone benches to left and right, either side of a square pool, all dating from the 15th century. Its water, now stagnant, was once believed to be a cure for·eye ailments.

Clynnog is much older than any of these medieval structures, a fact readily confirmed by walking down the lane beside the church. Ignore all exits right or left, and continue to the T-junction, where you should turn left and mount the five-step style to continue parallel to the sea. After a total walk of little more than half-a-mile (800m) one sees the well-preserved Bachwen burial chamber, or more accurately the now exposed cromlech stones of a megalithic chambered tomb, surrounded by an iron fence. The enormous capstone and three of its upright supports are about 3,000 years old, but one is surprised to find a shallow circular hole, left by a quarryman's pneumatic drill, in the fourth upright. It transpires that this stone was replaced early last century by the Honourable F.G. Wynn, of Glynllifon.

Back on the Caernarfon-Pwllheli road, a cottage is inscribed: 'Hwn oedd tŷ Eben Fardd', and indeed it was the home of poet, teacher and postmaster, Ebenezer Thomas. I enjoyed lunch at the Coach Inn (once called St Beuno's). There is another hostelry, the Clynnog, a short distance up the road.

(AUGUST 1994)

COLWYN BAY

The Welsh Mountain Zoo

THE Welsh Mountain Zoo is far more than a collection of animals. Before becoming a zoo the wooded Flagstaff estate was shrouded in mystery, a place rarely seen after the 1909 proclamation of the following year's National Eisteddfod at Colwyn Bay.

The Gorsedd circle for that event dominates a knoll now used for falconry displays, and is just one of the zoo's many unusual facets. When the Gorsedd returned to Colwyn Bay in 1910, Archdruid Dyfed apologised for the circle's distance from the pavilion.

'The Gorsedd events of Eisteddfod week will therefore be held on Rydal fields,' he said, adding: 'But the stones placed for last year's proclamation at Y Fanerig will remain for ever, a memorial to the Colwyn Bay National Eisteddfod.'

Fanerig is a translation that has probably not been heard since for what older residents still describe as The Flagstaff, a strange name dating back to 1887, when the vantage point was used to warn Mochdre anti-tithe farmers of the approach of law-enforcing police and troops.

It was in the 1890s that Dr Walter Whitehead, then in his 50s, thought he had found himself a bride and set about planning a home for her on the 37 acre Flagstaff estate. Professor Thomas H. Mawson, designer of some of the world's most famous gardens, and his architectural partner Dan Gibson, were commissioned to develop the site. Their 1898 plan shows a large house at the end of a 400 yard (360m) long drive. The drive is still there, and so are the gardens, but the house was never built. Legend has it that when the bride-to-be was brought to survey the site of her future home she was frightened by the eeriness of the remote and lonely spot, and fled back to the more familiar streets of Manchester.

For whatever reason, Dr Whitehead never married and only the gatehouse, now the Zoo office, was built of Gibson's grand plan. Mawson said in his memoirs that Dr Whitehead swindled them of their fees. The Italian gardens, rockeries and lily ponds were designed by a Llandudno Junction gardener, William Lee, who wrote to me nearly half-a-century ago describing how he spent twenty-seven years on the estate after Dr Whitehead's death in 1913.

The doctor's tomb is another unusual feature one does not expect to find in a zoo. Not very obvious, it is beside the path beyond the present penguin pool. It records that he was president of the BMA in 1903 and was nearly 73 when he died. The tomb contains a casket of his ashes together with those of a nameless eccentric German who shared Whitehead's home in the gatehouse.

The two men built what was meant to represent the bridge of a ship, complete with portholes, wall bunks and mast. Wearing sailor's caps, they would spend hours together, surveying the then very busy Liverpool Bay with telescopes. Part of their fantasy survives in what is now the Lookout Cafe.

A plaque on the bridge over Lee's lily pond commemorates the zoo's founder, Robert Jackson, who was killed in 1969 when a tree fell on him while he was fishing.

(MAY 1993)

COLWYN BAY

Station Road

COLWYN BAY's Station Road, once a Mecca for north Wales shoppers seeking elegance and quality, may end its days as a street market, a recent twice-weekly innovation. Station Road was in decline by 1961 when three architects, Sir Clough Williams-Ellis, Leonard Moseley and S. Powell Bowen,

Porth Amlwch

Mynydd Parys, Amlwch

Bala

Biwmares castle from the air

Offa's Dyke

Bethesda chapel in Bethesda

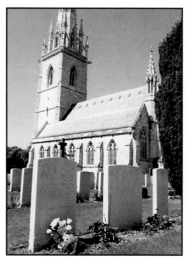

'The Marble Church', Bodelwyddan

Fflint castle

The Roman fort of Segontium, Caernarfon

'Y Porth Mawr', Caernarfon

'Y Maes', Caernarfon

Caernarfon town, looking down on the castle and Cei Llechi – the quay that exported Welsh slate all over the world

Snowdon from Capel Curig

Plas y Brenin, Capel Curig

Chirk Castle

71

Clynnog Fawr

Llywelyn the Great is honoured at Lancaster Square, Conwy

Deganwy

Denbigh's High Street

Dinllugwy

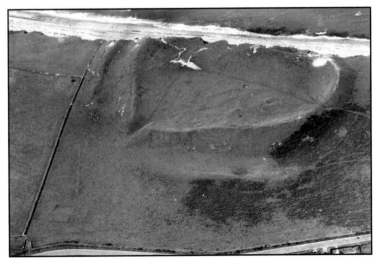

Dinas Dinlle

Dolwyddelan's castle, one of the last of the Welsh strongholds

Y Felinheli from the air

Holyhead harbour

Old Irish Mail steamers at Holyhead harbour

The 'holy well' at Holywell

An old photograph of the Marquess column at Llanfairpwllgwyngyll

Ynys Llanddwyn

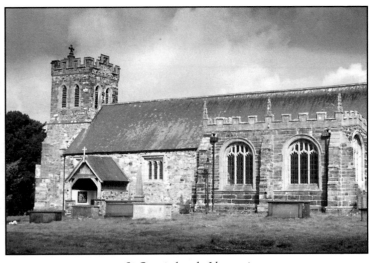

St Grwst church, Llanrwst

Nefyn town on the northern shore of Llŷn

Penmon

Porthdinllaen

Portmeirion

proposed a £7,000 rescue, based on the 1958 co-ordinated facelift which had given new life to Norwich's Magdalen Street.

All that came out of the Colwyn Bay plan was the unnecessary 1964 removal (and destruction) of an interesting drinking fountain and gas lamp at the top of the hill, presented in 1895 by John Porter, the town's principal architect. It went to improve traffic flow, but the road was semi-pedestrianised in 1988.

Central Hotel, at the top of the road, was originally the Station Hotel, being visible across the open field separating it from the railway station at the bottom of the hill. Next is an 1892 example of Porter's work (in association with Lawrence Booth and Thomas Chadwick). This is a row of nine shops in glazed red brick, eight with peaked gables and the ninth with a tower, all built by Edward Foulkes.

The original Victorian canopy of W.H. Smith & Son still contains stained-glass representations of Chaucer, Shakespeare, Dante and Dickens, restored after being used as stone-throwing targets by some beer-soaked louts about a decade ago. High on one of the gables is a reminder that it was once the Post Office. Colwyn Bay's original postal address was 'near Conway'. The first Post Office was in a small shop in Conwy Road, from where a lone postman covered an area extending from Llysfaen to Mochdre. It was also located in Abergele Road and Penrhyn Road, moving in 1926 to a smart neo-Georgian building in Princes Drive, which closed in 1994, when the main Post Office moved into a supermarket built on the site of the old railway goods yard.

Most important of all the Station Road inscriptions are those on the tower above the relatively new pub called Liberty's: Colwyn Bay and Pwllycrochan Estate Company, Denbighshire County Council, National Provincial Bank of England, and Colwyn Bay & Colwyn Local Board, all of whom once shared the building. It was the 1865 sale of the Pwllycrochan Estate which created the new town of Colwyn Bay beside the Chester and Holyhead Railway. Carved decoration arched over the side door incorporates a pair of handcuffs, scales of justice and a chain, a reminder of Colwyn Bay's first police station, which was raided in 1995 by police looking for an alleged brothel in a massage parlour that had opened on the first floor!

At the bottom of the road the attractive clock tower was erected in 1989, in memory of an adventurous local man who died at the age of 34. Tragically, another memorial plaque had to be added to the base in memory of a craftsman who was fatally injured in a fall while erecting the clock.

The corner shop near the clock was Uxbridge House, the road's first grocer. Boots is a 1979 utilitarian replacement for a once-famous and well-designed draper's shop, Neville & Co. Even more famous was the big furniture shop of Daniel Allen, in mock-Tudor style. It closed in 1971 when the founder's grandson said he would not ruin the family's reputation by selling the inferior products of modern manufacturers.

The outwardly attractive Peacock's store, at the top of the road, was once the most famous shop of all. It was designed in 1933 by local architect and honorary Freeman of the Borough Sidney Colwyn Foulkes (son of Edward, the builder), for William S. Wood, whose monogram survives in the bronze flower boxes at first floor level.

(APRIL 1992)

CONWY

After the tunnel

CONWY is for sale! That is the inevitable conclusion to be drawn from a stroll through the depressingly obtrusive array of estate agents' signs in this gem of a walled town, ten years after the opening of the £190 million tunnel bypass. To add to the town's commercial problems its once cheap and commodious central car park was prettified by the local authority in 1994, with the consequential loss of a third of the available parking spaces, a huge increase in charges, and a hefty penalty for overstaying one's welcome by a minute or two.

The car park was created a quarter of a century ago out of an enormous 700 years old Vicarage garden dating from medieval times. While tourists seem content to pay the minimum parking fee, it is proving an unacceptable surcharge on a brief shopping errand. Day-trippers would be well advised to invest in more than the minimum two-hour fee, for it takes a lot longer than that to explore this interesting town.

An alternative long-stay car park beside the Llanrwst road is signposted, for those able to climb the steps, or make a long inclined detour if handicapped, to enter the town through the medieval Mill Gate, into Rose Hill street (corrupted through the centuries from the original Horse Mill street).

Wherever one parks, one might spend a few moments outside the Mill Gate, admiring some early public water closets. There is a row of twelve monumental structures designed high into this section of the town wall in 1283, when the now diverted Afon Gyffin tributary of Afon Conwy ran immediately below.

Until 1991 the narrow streets of Conwy had to accommodate all the traffic of the A55 North Wales coast road. The new-found freedom from noise and fumes comes as a mixed blessing in the deserted town. In 1994 Peter Dymond, executive director of Project Conwy, saw no decline but rather a 20pc increase in general business and a substantial increase in tourism since the opening of the tunnel.

'We got down to six empty shops at one stage but now have more than twenty, for which we have four or five potential retailers and perhaps ten craft units in the old Wheelhouse Restaurant,' he said. 'An old bank in High Street is being converted into a Harrod's style quality food store,' said Mr Dymond, but conceded the developer would then close his existing high quality shop, across the road, which was what happened.

Unfortunately Project Conwy was then in the process of winding itself up, at the end of its planned four-year Government-funded operation to encourage the enhancement of the town, during the construction and opening of the tunnel.

'We were good value for money, costing only £300,000 but generating £15.4m of investment in the town,' added Mr Dymond.

There is abundant evidence of the investment, most noticeably in Lancaster Square, which has been remodelled as a pedestrian area, around the old fountain and statue of Llywelyn ap Iorwerth, presented to the town in 1898 by Albert Wood, of Bodlondeb, who made his money manufacturing anchor chains for such ships as the *SS Great Britain*.

His Conwy home, built in 1877, was extended in 1991 and opened by the Queen as the offices of Aberconwy Borough Council, which in 1996 was merged with Colwyn Borough Council and various other bits of north Wales to create a new all-purpose authority called Conwy County Borough.

(APRIL 1994)

CROESOR

Saved from drowning

ONCE scheduled for drowning in the bottom reservoir of a proposed pumped storage hydroelectric generating scheme, the Croesor valley lives in rural isolation. The village of some two-score houses, scattered at the end of a glacial cul-de-sac, owes its existence to Victorian attempts to mine a fortune from the slate hidden deep within Moelwyn (mountain), which glowers down on the community.

Its name, however, is much older, old enough to be attributed to the 3rd century Roman Empress Helen, who was said to have exclaimed 'Croes awr!' *(ill-fated hour!)*, when seeing her son fatally wounded here by a Welshman's poisoned arrow.

Residents of Croesor have always been slow to welcome strangers, and the poisoned arrow is plausible, but we need a better explanation for the origins of the name. It is unlikely that the Iberian or Balkan born Helen (authorities cannot agree which) opted to speak the Welsh tongue as her first language, despite her imperial years at York, from where her husband ruled as Emperor in the West. Furthermore her son made an epic ride from Wales to become Constantine the Great, founder of Byzantium.

The nearest Croesor ever got to a Byzantine Christian edifice was its Presbyterian chapel, built in 1865. Its impressive facade, once worthy of ancient Rome, still dominates the village, but closer inspection reveals it has been truncated from the rear, to a size more compatible with its twenty members. I was fortunate enough to find the chapel door open in 1991, with 76-years-old Miss Gwenedith Rowlands inside, preparing it for Sunday worship. She had been the chapel organist for fifty-three years and caretaker for many years. Miss Rowlands moved to Croesor in 1926 when her father was appointed headmaster of the village school, which still has twenty pupils.

Her mother used to keep the village shop and Post Office, which Miss Rowlands remembers in four different premises, until the last one closed in 1990. Today there is no commerce, no goods or services to be bought or sold here, but oddly enough, it still attracts new residents.

'The last of our slate mines closed in 1930, when Moses Kellow left for Cheltenham – that's his old house, Bryn,' said Miss Rowlands, as she pointed far up the valley, into the bowl nestling between Cnicht and Moelwyn. The Kellow hydraulic rotary rock-drill, invented at Croesor in 1899, was once famous throughout the world, but it is for his introduction of hydro-electricity to his quarry that Moses Kellow is commemorated on a group of primitively carved slate slabs of local history, opposite the school.

Bibliophile 'Bob Owen, Croesor' (1885-1962), best known of all the village's sons, is commemorated on a slate seat built into the wall of the chapel, where he was an elder. In its heyday Croesor had its own railway, opened in 1864 to carry its slate to Porthmadog. The last rails were lifted in 1949 but one can still pick out parts of the track-bed.

(APRIL 1991)

CWM-Y-GLO

An explosive past

CWM-Y-GLO sat astride the road linking Llanrug and Llanberis until isolated in obscurity by the 1973 bypass, which came with the construction of Dinorwig power station. Its name seems to mean 'valley of coal' but, with no coal in the area, one has to seek another explanation. The late Professor Bedwyr Lewis Jones once told me that Cwm-y-glo had exactly the same ancient origin as Gloddaeth, the Llandudno mansion of the Mostyn family, now better known as St David's College.

Glo, the Welsh word now used exclusively for coal, originally meant charcoal, for which the modern word is golosg which, in an intermediate stage, meant coke. Cwm-y-glo took its name from the charcoal makers who created the hamlet.

Its location gave it new life towards the end of the 18th century as the landing place for roofing slates, ferried either from Glynrhonwy farm, at the top end of Llyn Padarn, or from what became Dinorwig quarry, on the opposite side of the lake. Slates were transferred to carts for carriage to the port of Caernarfon, but the same carts also carried goods in the opposite direction. One such cargo nearly destroyed the community in 1869, in an explosion that changed the law on the importation and carriage of nitroglycerine.

Invented in 1846 by Ascanio Sobrero, nitroglycerine was obsolete by the time five tons of the heavy oil turned up at Caernarfon in 1869. Alfred Nobel invented the safer mixture he called dynamite in 1862, but continued to make 'blasting oil' near Hamburg, whose ships were in regular trade with the north Wales slate ports after the fire that destroyed the city in 1842, to create a new roofing market.

Thus two carts, each containing a ton of delicate explosive needing protection from heat and vibration, set off from Caernarfon, and the story of what happened to them is told in *Death blast in Snowdonia*, written by my school contemporary Meirion Hughes.

The carts exploded soon after leaving Cwm-y-glo, where they had stood in the sun, first outside the Blue Bell, now converted into a pair of garages next-door to Tanymarian, and then at the Alexandra, now a house. Both drivers and three bystanders were killed and eight people were seriously injured. All that was left of the carts was a wheel, found with harness half-a-mile away, 400 feet (122m) up the slopes of Cefn Du, at a spot still marked by a stone, off the road which leads to Bryn Bras Castle.

Bryn Bras is Cwm-y-glo's unexpected gem, to which the owners, Neville and Marita Gray Parry, admit visitors during the holiday season. Built during 1830-35 by Bangor solicitor Tom Williams, it was soon extended to the design of Thomas Hopper, architect of Kinmel, Erddig and Penrhyn Castle. There were further extensions after a fire in 1862. Subsequent owners added wood panelling spanning four centuries and coming from many sources, but blending it remarkably well to make an elegant house of manageable proportions.

(AUGUST 1994)

DEGANWY

Forgotten castle

AN OCCASIONAL bleating sheep in the meadow below, or the less frequent attenuated clatter of a distant train, are the only sounds you will hear from Castell Deganwy. Offering one of the world's finest 360 degree panoramas, this forgotten cauldron of Welsh history remains unpolluted by so much as a discarded cigarette stump.

Its surviving battlements are a mixture of fortifications built, destroyed and rebuilt: by the Normans under Robert de Rhuddlan in 1080; by the Normans again under the Earl of Chester in 1210; by the Welsh under Llywelyn ap Iorwerth in 1213; by the Normans/English of Henry III in 1244; and by the Welsh of Llywelyn ap Gruffudd in 1257. The missing stones may now be seen on the other side of the river, recycled by Edward I in the building of Conwy town walls.

Deganwy Castle's story goes back much further than that. It was the Castro Deganno where St Bride of Kildare (also known as St Brigit and St Ffraed or Ffraid) was said to have landed round about the year 500. By 517 it was the seat of government of Maelgwn Gwynedd, and it was here, according to tradition, that he founded the Welsh eisteddfod, designed to separate the true minstrels from the plague of wandering vagabonds. Unable to select the winning minstrel by ear, Maelgwn ordered them to decide the issue with a fiendish swimming race across the treacherous Deganwy narrows, below his castle. Most of the wretched competitors were, presumably, last seen drifting past the castle, and even today one is tempted to think this might be a good way of reducing Wales's surfeit of druids and minstrels!

To find this now tranquil memorial to the warriors of yore, drive up York Road, turning off Deganwy's main road. Wind your way up the hill until you find the 'public footpath' sign on your left, from where you will have to walk for only a quarter of an hour. At the end of the short walled path there is a wishing gate, beyond which there is a choice of three paths: to the left, straight ahead, or over a stile to the right.

The castle is atop the formidable-looking cliffs on your left, for which you need to take the middle path. After six to eight minutes you will arrive at the ruins of an ancient gate house, on which there is a modern descriptive slate plaque, in Welsh and English. Continue along the path, which follows the contours in a remarkably easy walk to the summit, but do keep firm control of any children who may be with you.

First soak in the magnificent views embracing Conwy and the whole of the Conwy estuary; the Snowdonia foothills, Menai Strait and the whole of Conwy Bay; Ynys Seiriol *(Puffin Island)*, and much of Ynys Môn round to Point Lynas; the whole of Llandudno, most of Rhos-on-Sea, with Liverpool Bay, Blackpool and the Cumbrian hills beyond; and the whole of Llansanffraid-Glan Conwy, whose full name preserves the dedication to St Bride.

The old war lords certainly knew where to build a desirable residence. A surprising amount still stands of the erstwhile lodgings of such distinguished travellers as King John, Archbishop Baldwin and Giraldus Cambrensis (recruiting for the Crusades), Llywelyn ap Iorwerth, Llywelyn ap Gruffudd and King Henry III (contemplating his defeat).

(SEPTEMBER 1990)

DINBYCH (DENBIGH)

The town walls

DENBIGH *(Dinbych)* town walls are one of Wales's best kept secrets, said architects engaged in 1990 to enhance the old town's tourist image. I can but agree, for they are almost impossible to find – unless you happen to be looking up at them from Howell's School.

Designed to protect the original medieval town, the mighty walls were built at the end of the 13th century, simultaneously with the construction of the castle which still crowns the hill dominating Dyffryn Clwyd. The old town clung to the steep hillsides, and was abandoned in the 15th century for the slightly flatter site of present-day Denbigh, since when the burgesses seem never to have looked over their corporate shoulder.

'Please can you show me the way to the town walls?' I asked of the shoppers in Denbigh's busy High Street, with its 16th century County Hall. I tried it in English, and I tried it in Welsh, and was directed here, there and everywhere, but not to Wales's best kept secret. Most people referred me to the Burgess Gate, tucked away at the end of Broomhill Lane out of High Street. With its twin drum towers and arched entrance it is part of the original town walls, but obviously not what I was seeking.

Eventually some children told me to take the path hidden in the dip to the left of the castle entrance, over the stile at the end, across the lane, through the wishing gate, and then go down into the woods. 'You'll see the big wall in front of you,' they assured me.

Even finding the picturesque castle is a navigational feat worthy of a Boy Scout badge, for it vanishes behind a network of narrow lanes once one has arrived in the town. Having first found the castle I followed the children's instructions, and did indeed come to the town walls – behind a padlocked gate. Retracing my steps, I called at the castle where the friendly custodian told me that I (and anyone else) could borrow the keys for a modest £1 deposit. I took up the offer, and followed directions to the opposite end of the wall walk, beside the unfinished Leicester's Church which was intended to be a 16th century replacement for St Asaph Cathedral.

Construction stopped when Robert Dudley, Earl of Leicester and Lord of Denbigh, favourite of Queen Elizabeth, and the most powerful man in north Wales, died in 1588. Money squeezed out of the people of north Wales in order to complete the church was 'borrowed' in 1599 by the Earl of Essex, on his way to Ireland with sixteen thousand troops to deal with any tax evaders.

Denbigh never saw its money again, but was left with the present impressive unfinished ruins. To their left there is a ramp leading to another obscure gate, which is also padlocked. Here, at last, was Denbigh's hidden secret, a delightful walk along ancient battlements interspersed with three interesting towers. But it is the views of Dyffryn Clwyd, across the surprisingly extensive playing fields of Howell's School, that make the whole expedition worthwhile. It was in Dinbych that I first went to school, but I never heard so much as a mention of this extraordinary vista. At least today's schoolchildren know where it is.

(AUGUST 1990)

DINLLUGWY

A Stone Age city

FOR a quick induction course in ancestral perseverance, ingenuity and strength, visit Dinllugwy, at Penrhosllugwy in Ynys Môn *(Anglesey)*. The roads are narrow and parking is difficult, so visit before or after summer holidaymakers arrive or depart.

First stop off at Llugwy burial chamber, which is beside the road, and try to figure out how Stone Age man lifted the 25-ton capstone into place. It is more than 18 feet (5.5m) long, 16 feet (4.9m) wide, and over a yard (1m) thick; and was carefully placed to form the roof on a burial chamber of upright stones, with its entrance facing east. The tomb, which contained the remains of thirty men, women and children, when excavated in 1908, was built about 4,500 years ago, while the Egyptians were building their enormous pyramids in the Nile Valley.

A few hundred yards/metres down the road there is an ill-advised attempt at political correctness that is equally confusing to Welsh and English readers. It appears to be pointing to the roofless ruins of a medieval church, in the adjoining field, and that is all that most visitors ever see. Forget the church, for the present, and head across the field, beside the boundary fence on the left, into the wooded mound beyond. Hidden among the trees is an amazing stone-built Old-Welsh village coinciding with the closing years of the Roman occupation, of around 350 AD. Stones of enormous proportions have been used to build two circular and seven rectangular houses, all within a town wall 5 feet (1.5m) thick. Some of the stones are 10 feet (3.3m) long and the walls stand to heights varying between 4 and 6 feet (1.2 and 1.8m), a truly remarkable sight.

It is conjectured that it must have been the fortified homestead of a chieftain. When the site was excavated in 1905 three coins of Constantine the Great (320 AD) and two of slightly later age were found. There was also a twisted bronze bracelet. Pottery, which appeared to originate in the New Forest, had been carefully repaired with iron rivets, suggesting that such utensils were difficult to obtain in 4th century Ynys Môn. The repairs also demonstrated considerable skill in a community which had by then been living in the area for about 3,000 years.

On the way back to the road, walk across to the ancient church with its south chapel added in the 16th century. Steps lead down into a vault 8 feet (2.4m) square, discovered early in the 19th century when a fox was being dug out. Everyone looking out to sea from this spot is intrigued by the tower on nearby Ynys Dulas, which is the foul-smelling visible third of a treacherous reef. The tower was built in 1824 by Colonel James Hughes, as an unlit warning to passing shipping.

When the bride of the 5th baronet, Sir Thomas Neave,

arrived at Llys Dinas, in 1908, she was told of shipwrecks on the island as recently as 1902 and 1903, and she took to having the tower stocked with food, water and coal for the use of marooned sailors.

(JUNE 1991)

DINAS DINLLE

Caernarfon's Southend

DINAS DINLLE was meant to be to Caernarfon what Southend is to London, but never managed to develop into more than one three-storey hotel (now holiday flats) and a couple of dozen houses, many still with their original corrugated asbestos roofs. Its beach offers lots of good sand and officially designated clean bathing water, but it cannot be seen from the parallel road because of the very necessary bank of shingle storm defences that prevent rough seas from submerging the low-lying houses.

A concrete promenade, some 4 feet (1.2m) wide, once topped the shingle but most of it has collapsed, to add to Dinas Dinlle's neglected appearance, for which there does not appear to be any improvement plan. Yet the beach has recently become very popular at weekends, and one cannot fail to notice that nearly all its users speak Welsh with the unmistakable Caernarfon accent. It is now nearer to becoming Caernarfon's Southend-on-Sea than ever before, if someone would only invest a bit of money in the place.

Its name informs us that Dinas Dinlle has been inhabited and fortified for at least 2,000 years, but the old stepped path into the ancient hill fort has been sealed off with barbed wire, presumably because the headland is gradually collapsing into the sea. But Dinas Dinlle's erosion problem has been discussed for nearly two centuries. In 1880 Caernarfon Harbour Trustee W.A. Darbishire, well known for his artistic talent, painted the beach scene, showing extensive protective sand dunes. In 1915 he took his painting to a meeting of the trustees to emphasise the loss of at least 30 yards (27m) of land for a length of 7,500 yards (6850m), but World War One got in the way and Caernarfon never returned to the problem of sea defence works.

Roman coins spanning the period 253-296 AD have been found in the hill fort, into the base of which there was sunk a more substantial fort in 1940, linked to another nearer the beach, to defend Dinas Dinlle against the perceived threat of a German invasion.

There have been many shipwrecks on this shore, including a full-rigged Spanish vessel towards the end of the 18th century, two of whose guns survived until recently at Fort Belan and Glynllifon.

'There was great loss of life and treasure; I have often heard my father and mother speak of it. They drove down to see the place and witnessed the sad spectacle of numerous bodies,' noted Sir Llewelyn Turner, mayor of Caernarfon during 1859-70. It brought about the ruin of the Llandwrog village tailor who, at a very low tide, collected several gold coins in the vicinity of the wreck. Abandoning his former industrious ways, he spent his ill-gotten fortune on drink and ended his days in the poorhouse.

A Caernarfon man's third attempt to emigrate to Australia in an ex-Army amphibious DUKW landing craft named *Welsh Endeavour* ended at Dinas Dinlle in 1971. He was given a great send-off, to a cacophony of motor horns from the town's slate quay, but after only five miles of his intended 12,000 mile voyage the *Welsh Endeavour* was wrecked on a sand bank. At his first attempt he got as far as France before being forced back to Caernarfon for engine repairs. On his second attempt he was towed back from the English Channel.

(JUNE 1993)

DOLWYDDELAN

Llywelyn's birthplace

DOLWYDDELAN takes its name from St Gwyddelan who established a church here sometime around 600. It is the only meadow within the steep-sided Dyffryn Lledr, and Gwyddelan's llan *(enclosure)* was on the central hill now known as Bryn y Bedd *(Hill of the grave)*. More permanent churches followed until the site was abandoned in about 1500, when the present St Gwyddelan's church was built on the meadow. Its interesting historic interior is still in regular use for services, but the church is otherwise kept locked.

A poignant gravestone tells of how the 13-years-old son of the traction engine superintendent was killed, beneath the wheels of the engine, during the cutting of the railway tunnel to Blaenau Ffestiniog in 1877. The old church is hidden from the busy A470 Llandudno-Cardiff road, where modern travellers see only St Elizabeth's, built in 1884 for non-Welsh-speakers, and recently converted into two houses.

Dolwyddelan's picturesque Welsh built castle dominates the route from Dyffryn Conwy into Mid Wales. Traditionally this is where Llywelyn ap Iorwerth (the Great) was born in 1173. It was Llywelyn who built the first two storeys of today's magnificent keep, which was given an extra floor at the end of the 15th century.

First calling at the farm, to buy a ticket, one can visit the keep via a short but steep walk through indigenous trees and undergrowth. It probably looks much the same as it did in Llywelyn's days, and was recently used as the set for a film about Robin Hood's escapades in Nottinghamshire. The keep contains an illustrated introduction to Welsh medieval history, leading up to the capture of Dolwyddelan by Edward I, on 18 January 1283. Views from the battlements are superb, northwards down Dyffryn Lledr, southwards up Bwlch Gogerddan *(the Crimea Pass)*, eastwards to the village, and westwards to Moel Siabod, on the far side of which an Aer Lingus Dakota crashed in 1952, with the loss of 23 lives.

Opposite the castle, at the entrance of Tan-Castell farm, the enormously vulgar red marble column is in memory of four Calvinistic Methodist brothers, 'three ministers and one elder,' who were born at the farm between 1796 and 1805. Although they preached entirely in Welsh, their memorial was inscribed entirely in English, so as to ensure that the entire world knew of their 'eloquence, music, theology, poetry'.

A later slate slab, attached to the other side of the house, gives further details in Welsh, reminding us that one of the brothers was more famous than the rest, as 'John Jones, Talysarn'. It also lists their otherwise unknown sisters: Margared, Catherine, Mary, Gwen and Jane.

The slab is a reminder that Dolwyddelan's economy switched briefly from agriculture to slate quarrying in the 19th century. Now much disguised by nature, the abandoned quarries (there were several) can be reached by walking past the ancient church and over Pont y Llan, the bridge that spans Afon Lledr's salmon spawning beds. An inscribed stone on the bridge gives the date 1808 and the names of J. Defford, surveyor and 'Io Owen'.

Wales's only handmade bone china pottery factory (with tea shop) can be found in the old school, behind the church.

(AUGUST 1991)

DYSERTH

Waterfall in the High Street

THE community of Dyserth has been in existence for longer than anyone knows, but offers strangers no hint of its antiquity. Where else can one find a magnificent waterfall in the high street? Winter defoliation of the intervening trees enables one to see, as well as hear it, but to view the cascade at its best you have to pay a few pence into the money-box at the gate. A walk of but a few paces then enables us to peer into the stone funnel, which the primeval vortex carved for itself when the flow was obviously very much greater.

If further evidence is needed of the river's past glory, cross the little footbridge (which is always veiled in fine spray) and mount the one hundred and twelve steps beyond. A splendid gorge is revealed at the top of the falls. For summer enjoyment a few more steps up the hill lead to three picnic tables and seats – but keep a firm grip on the children.

From here one can see a disused quarry, which is presumed to have eradicated any traces of the earliest community centred upon the vanished Dyserth castle. Probably starting as an ancient Brythonic frontier post that was castellated by the Welsh and refortified by Henry III in 1241, Dyserth castle was destroyed by Llywelyn ap Iorwerth (the Great).

Back in the main street another footbridge leads towards the towerless church of St Bridget *(Santes Ffraid)*, which looks deceptively new, being an 1870-75 rebuild by Sir George Gilbert Scott. During a walk around the outside you can see it incorporates much older features, such as the lintel inscribed: 'Sr John Conway, Kngt, 1636," (one of the ancestors of Lord Langford, of Bodrhyddan). Dyserth church was indeed mentioned in the Domesday book of 1086, and the present building contains many relics of the past, including a medieval Celtic cross found being used as a stile. One of the roof timbers is inscribed with the date 1579 and Queen Elizabeth's cipher, the initials of the notoriously avaricious Bishop William Hughes, and of the unidentified 'DH'. Substantial remains of an ancient Jesse tree are incorporated in the east window, which was rebuilt in 1875 at the expense of the Bodrhyddan family, who inserted their coat of arms. The oldest glass contains the date 1450 (in Roman numerals), and the name of the then absentee Archdeacon of St Asaph and Vicar of Dyserth, John Tubney, of Rochester.

An old people's home, across the road from the church, is the former twenty-two-bedroom vicarage, in which the incumbents of Dyserth shivered until 1968, when the Church in Wales conceded defeat in the battle against dampness, and decided to build the present fine Vicarage (which was not completed until December 1970). If one looks long enough at the new and all-enveloping paint on the old Vicarage one can find two plaques, the oldest telling us (in Latin) that it was built in 1584 by Bishop William Hughes, who was also Vicar of Dyserth, for which reason the house served as the St Asaph diocese Bishop's Palace until 1795.

A more unusual conversion, near the top of the hill, has a plaque telling us it is the Methodist chapel built in 1896, but whose modern door-knocker and letterbox convey a different message.

(FEBRUARY 1991)

EFYRNWY

Wales's biggest lake

LLYN EFYRNWY *(Vyrnwy)*, at the north-western corner of Powys close to the Gwynedd boundary, is Wales's biggest lake. It stretches for five miles (8km) through the Berwyn mountains and is surrounded by a road 12 miles (19km) long, in an Alpine-like setting. It is all man-made, the lake by Liverpool Corporation and the trees by the Forestry Commission, but it has been densely colonised by wildlife to create one of Britain's best sites administered by the Royal Society for the Protection of Birds.

A massive yet picturesque dam, 100 feet (30m) high, holds back the lake. Travellers and students of the famous RAF dambuster squadron of 1943 will be struck by its architectural similarity to Germany's Möhne Dam, each with ornamental towers straddling the road along the lip.

Efyrnwy is the older of the two. Plaques at the eastern end tell something of its history, starting with the Liverpool Waterworks Act, 1880. The first stone was laid by the Earl of Powys in 1881 and the dam was completed seven years later, when the valves were closed to start flooding the valley. Completion of the scheme was not celebrated until 1910 when Edward, Prince of Wales, turned up to unveil another plaque. Yet another completion was celebrated in 1938. Work on its German look-alike did not begin until 1905.

The Efyrnwy dam is 390 yards (360m) long, 40 yards (36) wide at the base, tapering to a carriageway 20 yards (18m) wide at the top, and running over thirty-three arches through which flood waters sometimes overflow in an impressive cascade. Some distance away the draw-off tower stands 113 above the surface, romantically fashioned like a Bavarian castle, to conceal its most remarkable engineering feature: the start of a tunnel more than two miles long, from where the water is piped to Prescott.

Modern commerce is such that this Welsh water, drunk in Liverpool by customers of North West Water actually belongs to Severn Trent Water, whose regional offices are at the western end of the dam, in the new community of Llanwddyn. A reminder of the original village of the same name is inscribed in Welsh on the wall of the former Bethel Presbyterian chapel, telling us it was built in 1874, moved from the village in 1888, and rebuilt in 1889. The original village, and its church with ancient links to the Hospitaller Knights of St. John, was destroyed by dynamite as the waters began to rise to create the artificial lake. Its street pattern and foundations survive 35 feet (11m) beneath the surface of the lake.

All this basic information about the origins of the lake is somewhat difficult to find at the Severn Trent information centre, housed in the old chapel, where there is an exhibition touching upon some of the legends of the area, though not in a way those familiar with old Montgomeryshire might recognise.

However the centre does have some very useful literature on the nature trails that start there, and which include bird hides. Age has given respectability to man's interference with the environment, resulting in a haven blessed with the Lake Vyrnwy Hotel.

(JULY 1993)

EGLWYSBACH

A place of date stones

EGLWYSBACH in Dyffryn Conwy is a happy blend of attractive old buildings and sympathetically-designed new houses, spoilt only by the starkly unmistakable local authority in-filling of the 1930s. Philologists would argue for the name to be mutated to Eglwysfach, like a village of that spelling in Ceredigion, but that assumes they both mean 'little church', or church in a place anciently referred to as being 'the small', or 'the lesser'.

The mutated topographical version is to be found inside the parish church, in the Latin inscription 'Ecclesia de Fach', on the 1846 memorial to Howell Holland Edwards of Pennant, a canon of Westminster and founder of the now-demolished St Mary's church, in Llanrwst.

However, the 'b' spelling persists, in the belief that it is derived from the name of a 7th century local chieftain, Bach ap Carwed, whose home was on the site of the present church tower.

St Martin's church, a simple design by a Conwy man, was rebuilt in 1782, but the font and other parts are much older, and a board inside lists the vicars since 1537. A date-stone on the porch tells us it was added in 1837; another, on the churchyard wall, is dated 1858.

Eglwysbach is rich in date stones, from which we see that

most of the ancient-looking buildings were put up only in the 19th century. The village school, dated 1835, was architecturally inspired for its period, giving the children a bright environment. Tyddyn-y-llan Terrace is dated 1872; the house next door 1894. The date 1895 is just visible on the facade of Dolwar, preserved only by an accumulation of paint layers beneath the present blanket coating, and begging for picking out in new paint.

Across the street Islwyn is dated 1847, together with the initials 'JB', but there is no date on the interesting-looking village institute next door. This used to be the Bodnod Arms, which lost its inn licence in 1909 when the magistrates decided it was redundant. It is probably the oldest building in the street, and took its name from the original spelling of nearby Bodnant, the home since 1875 of Lord Aberconway's family. The old form of the estate name is shown in the church, on the memorial stone of John Forbes, who fought the American revolutionaries in 1777, as an officer of the 40th Foot (later styled the 2nd Somerset Regiment, and now part of the Queen's Lancashire Regiment). He married Mary Lloyd, heiress to Bodnod.

Redundancy has not yet befallen The Bee, next door to the village institute. Old though it looks, some of it is a Victorian extension of a much older tavern (as distinct from an inn). It was listed in the 1844 tithe schedule as the property of the Reverend Canon Howell Holland Edwards, already mentioned, and from whom it was once known as the Pennant Arms. There was yet a third tavern, the 17th century Sun, now a private house at the top of the hill as one enters the village.

(JANUARY 1993)

Y FELINHELI

The port of Dinorwig

FELINHELI was a place I knew particularly well when it was a thriving self-sufficient village that we called Port Dinorwig. Four decades later I found a bizarre blend of affluence and decay. Its two docks, built to export the slate which used to be conveyed by rail from Dinorwig quarries, are now home to a fortune in cabin cruisers and luxury yachts, yet the quayside looks as though it has been hit by a cluster bomb. The old quayside office, whose roof and walls demonstrate the skills of the old slate dresser, incorporating the purple, green and blue varieties once found in Dinorwig, has become a restaurant, albeit shut when I called.

Time stands still amid the empty shops in the high street, fixed at 5.42 on all four faces of the clock commemorating local men killed in the 1914-18 war. A plaque added after World War Two includes the name of Naval Lieutenant Thomas Lloyd-Jones, whose parents wanted him honoured on the cenotaph at Caernarfon. Caernarfon was his home town, which had been particularly well served by his father and grandfather, but a pedantic borough council ruled otherwise because the father had moved during the war to a new address just outside the borough boundary.

A plaque over the door of Llanfair-is-gaer Church House, next-door to the memorial, reminds us of yet another name for Y Felinheli. The handsome yellow brick building to the rear is the railway station, opened on St David's Day, 1852, by the Bangor & Caernarfon Railway Company, but closed in 1969. By the addition of an external wall its one platform has become an interior room of what is now a warehouse.

Felinheli was shared between two lots of magistrates until about 30 years ago, giving the village an hour's more drinking time than anywhere else. The Caernarfon Borough bench allowed pubs at the western end to remain open until 10pm, whereas the more temperate minded Caernarfon County magistrates, meeting in the same building, applied a 9pm closure to Halfway House, at the eastern end – which meant it could open an hour earlier than its rivals.

Halfway House, the one spark of refurbishment in the village, is now renamed the Welsh equivalent, Tŷ Hanner Ffordd, where I enjoyed my lunch listening to the Wenglish vernacular. Faenol, the once elegant house which dominated the economic development of the entire area, is a sorry sight, its once pristine walls stained by vegetation. Yet as recently as 1969, when it still used the phonetic English spelling of 'Vaynol', it housed the greatest gathering of the Royal family ever assembled under one roof outside a Royal palace. It was then the home of Sir Michael Duff, who was related to several strands of the Royal family, and was a close friend of the rest. His house was used by the family on the eve of the Investiture of Prince Charles at Caernarfon Castle.

Long before that Princess Marina, Duchess of Kent, had been a regular visitor to Faenol, from where she and Sir Michael and Lady Caroline Duff would sometimes slip away for a quiet excursions to the surrounding countryside.

Sir Michael's 25,000 acre estate, including the summit of Snowdon, was a gift from Queen Anne to his ancestor John Smith, who asked for land instead when offered a peerage in 1708. Sir Michael started selling it in 1967, and the rest went to meet death tax after 1980.

(JANUARY 1993)

FFESTINIOG

With the woman one loves . . .

FFESTINIOG, not to be confused with its Victorian industrial offspring called Blaenau Ffestiniog, is one of Wales's oldest communities. The area is usually associated with man-made mountains of slate waste, but that is not what one sees on arriving at the older village, which is often bypassed.

Ffestiniog, now more often called Llan Ffestiniog to distinguish it from its larger neighbour, supplied the original labour for the slate mines, two miles (3km) to the north, but remained a dormitory while Blaenau Ffestiniog grew, in the course of the last century, from a dozen smallholdings to a peak population of nearly eleven and a half thousand. It is now back down to under five and a half thousand.

Strangely, perhaps, one can still see why, when visiting Ffestiniog in 1756, poet and politician Lord Lyttleton wrote: 'If you have a mind to live long and renew your youth, come and settle in Ffestiniog. With the woman one loves, with the friend of one's heart, and a good study of books, one might pass an age in this vale and think it a day'.

Built at the head of the Vale of Ffestiniog, the village was once on the main road from Cardigan Bay to north-west Wales and Cheshire, before engineers had mastered such problems as Afon Conwy and the Crimea Pass. The Romans built a fort, with accompanying theatre, in the parish. The very impressive remains, known as Tomen y Mur, still stand. Narrow mountain roads have saved the site from the tramp of tourists' feet or a ticket collector.

In Crusader days Ffestiniog was on the pilgrims' road, south of the hospice of the Knights of St. John at Ysbyty Ifan. This tradition of caring for weary impecunious travellers was renewed in 1931 when, at the request of the Church in Wales, the Society of St Francis opened a friary in the big house called Bryn Llywelyn. It provided temporary accommodation and rehabilitation for periods of three to four months for wayfarers, which was the community's name for men who had become wandering begging tramps because of the unemployment conditions of that period. When their short lease expired, the friars moved to Cors-y-gedol, which they left in 1939 when the war absorbed all the unemployed. They reopened briefly at the old Llanrhos Rectory, Llandudno, in 1973. Their wooden carving of St Francis, originally made for Ffestiniog, is now housed at St Paul's church, Craig-y-don, Llandudno.

For much of the last century Ffestiniog was famous the length and breadth of Britain for its Morris Evans' Oil. The cure-all elixir was mixed in an old Caernarfon Militia hut, re-erected behind the petrol station on the Trawsfynydd road out of the village. Frank Evans, the last of the Ffestiniog 'oil sheikhs', died in 1974, aged 82. His house was called Bryn Olew (meaning oil hill), where it was once thought his father Morris had found a magic oil well in the garden. Ex-quarryman Morris Evans wanted to become a doctor, but had to make do with experiments in Welsh folk medicine. In 1905 David Lloyd George witnessed an affidavit that his concoction had cured some dreadful human disease, but the product's biggest boost came in 1910, when the *War Office Times and Naval Review* recommended Morris Evans' Oil as a horse medicine. That resulted in a big contract with Argentina.

(APRIL 1993)

FFLINT

A king's prison

FFLINT, which gave its name to the pre-1974 county of Flintshire (a name revived in 1996, though with different boundaries), is one of the oldest towns in Wales – or more accurately in the Palatinate of Chester, for the county was once the property of the Earl of Chester, a title which has belonged to the Prince of Wales since the 14th century.

Today's only vestige of Fflint's antiquity is its castle, the first to be built by Edward I during his conquest of north Wales. Work began on 25 July 1277, with a plan incorporating the castle's most famous feature. This was the independent Great Tower, or Donjon, copied from the Tour de Constance at Aigues Mortes, which Edward had seen on his way home from the Crusades. Four months later Edward signed a peace treaty with Llywelyn ap Gruffudd, and construction seems to have slowed down, for the castle was not completed until 1280, in time for Llywelyn's abrogation of the peace treaty in 1282. The Welsh besieged the castle but were finally defeated, after which the castle lost any significance until 1399 when, as Shakespeare tells us, Richard II was captured there and forced to abdicate, after Henry Bolingbroke 'came along the shore with all his host'.

Shakespeare was only partially correct for Richard was ambushed and captured at Penmaenhead near Colwyn Bay, after being tricked into leaving Conwy Castle. He was taken on to Fflint as a prisoner, there to meet Bolingbroke who forced his abdication, and resultant imprisonment at Pontefract, where he was murdered a year later.

Today one can stand on the castle walls beside the Dee estuary and imagine that medieval scene. Furthermore one can do it for free, there no longer being a ticket booth. This is presumably because the castle fails to attract enough visitors to pay the wages but, by the same token, there is no one to sell a guide book.

Unlike later Edwardian boroughs, Fflint was never contained within a wall, which may be why the town has lost its medieval character except for the grid pattern of its streets. Of these only Church Street, which originally led to the castle gate, has retained any significant commercial activity. As its name implies, before being severed by the railway in 1848, this street linked the castle to the garrison church whose site is preserved within the foundations of the present 1846-48 structure. Marginally more interesting inside than out, it contains several monuments to the Muspratt family, of Seaforth Hall, Liverpool, and Trelawny House and Cornist, in Fflint. One inscription tells us James Muspratt, born in 1793, was the founder of Britain's alkali trade. By the time the Muspratts arrived Fflint was already industrialised, notably with a busy lead smelter using local ore.

Its chemical industry later attracted Courtaulds, whose factory towered above the castle, but has now vanished. The houses built for its workers will always be known locally as the Courtaulds' estate.

In a post World War Two moment of municipal madness the old town council built three blocks of fifteen-storey flats between the castle and the town. They are architecturally incongruous not only in Fflint but also in the wider scene of north Wales. The present town council uses a municipal monstrosity of 1840 as the Town Hall designed, believe it or not, by John Welch. Supposed to resemble a French medieval gate house, strangers have often mistaken it for the castle.

(JUNE 1994)

FFYNNON BEUNO

Refuge of H.M. Stanley

FFYNNON BEUNO is a place name that occurs six times in Wales, but here we are concerned with the quaint community that takes its name from the water south of Tremeirchion. The spring rises in an ancient walled and gated bath, 15 feet (4.5m) long and 10ft 6ins (3.15m) wide, where it reaches a depth of 4ft (1.2m) before overflowing through the mouth of a carved stone head, built into the wall. In one corner, though no longer usable, are some ancient steps, indicating that the water was once revered as a holy source of cures for those who bathed in it.

The well now stands in the front garden of a roadside farmhouse which also preserves the name of Ffynnon Beuno, gilded on the glass of the front porch. This was the famous Ffynnon Beuno Inn, where the future journalist-explorer Sir Henry Morton Stanley, then 15, found refuge in 1856, after absconding from St Asaph Workhouse.

H.M. Stanley was the name he later took from his American benefactor after working his passage from Liverpool at the end of 1858. While at the Workhouse he was known as John Rowlands, one of several illegitimate children of Elizabeth Parry, of Denbigh, who lies buried in Bodelwyddan churchyard. Elizabeth Parry's sister Mary was the widowed licensee of the Ffynnon Beuno Inn, where she brewed some of her own beer, ran a shop and worked the adjoining smallholding. In his autobiography Stanley recorded his gratitude to Aunt Mary, for the happiest years of his youth.

'What labour could a small, ignorant boy give for such bounties? I trimmed hedges, attended the sheep, cleared the byre, fed the stock, swept the farmyard, cut and stacked the fuel, drove Dobbin to Rhyl Station for coal, or to Denbigh for beer, or to Mostyn for groceries,' he recorded.

Being an adventurous lad he would have explored the impressive cave in the rock face behind the house. When excavated, in 1886, it was found to contain bones of long-extinct animals, including the mammoth, lion, woolly rhino and spotted hyena. Nowadays its winter occupants are lesser horseshoe bats, which disappear each summer to breed in the roof spaces of nearby houses. I was fortunate enough to be shown the cave by Liz Pierce, of Ffynnon Beuno, who drew my attention to the unusual weeds growing near the entrance, including milk thistle, some of which are harvested by a local herbalist. 'An interesting explanation is that the plants might have been brought here for medicinal purposes by monks centred on St Beuno's well,' she said.

Across the road is Brynbella, a 1794 replacement for Bach-y-graig, the 1567 home of Sir Richard Clough. One of Clough's descendants, and heiress to the estate, Hester Lynch Salusbury, became the famous Mrs Thrale, friend of Dr Johnson whom she met in 1764. Bach-y-graig was already derelict when Johnson visited it on 30 July 1774, to record: 'The floors have been stolen, the windows are stopped. The house was less than I seemed to expect.' Mrs Thrale subsequently married Gabriele Piozzi who embarked upon building the present Brynbella (for further information see under 'Tremeirchion').

(JUNE 1991)

FFYNNONGROYW

Once a miners' village

FFYNNONGROYW was built around the well *(ffynnon)* of bright *(gloyw)* water which gives the village its name, as distinct from the even more distorted anglicised version on the boundary sign. The name was first recorded 200 years ago, but Llinegr, the name still used locally for the eastern end of the village, dates from medieval times, when its mill was taxed.

As might be expected, Well Lane, which starts at Llinegr and loops back to join the main street, leads to the well, but what a sorry sight it is. Instead of making an ornamental feature of the well an insensitive district council bolted its iron door and covered and drained its shallow overflow pool, in which villagers used to bathe their feet, believing the water had therapeutic value. Twmpath, an 18th century cottage which backs on to the main street at the junction with Well Lane, is the oldest surviving house, but its front is disappointing, having lost its character by modernisation.

Legend tells us that Ffynnongroyw was first colonised by

shipwrecked sailors who found the well, in the days when a ketch or small schooner would put to sea manned by only the master, his wife and a boy. Only in the 19th century did it become a convenient dormitory for men working at Point of Ayr colliery or Mostyn iron works. The enormous Miners' Institute, which once offered local families a wide range of recreational facilities, is now empty.

Most of the chapels have gone the same way. Still inscribed 'Tabernacl, Addoldy y Bedyddwyr', the 1892 Baptist chapel has been converted into three smart houses, with basement garages where the vestry used to be. Bethania Welsh Wesleyan Methodist church, founded in 1865 and rebuilt in 1912, is closed and for sale. Closed, too, is Moriah Welsh Presbyterian church, founded in 1848, but its members, like those from Bethania, now share Siloah with the Congregationalists, who built it in 1895 in Mornant Avenue, on land reclaimed from the sea. St Andrews, built by Victorian Congregationalists for the village's few non-Welsh speakers, now belongs to a minority evangelical sect. Next door is a boarded up building bearing two unusual carved inscriptions recording its 1871 origins as the village school. One says 'Nonedenominational' (with a superfluous 'e') and the other 'Undenominational'. The parish church, opened in 1882 (on land acquired for the purpose in 1847), is still in good shape. An unexpected feature is the use of a miner's safety lamp in the chancel, though the eternal light is now electrified. Also unusual, especially so close to the English border, is the use of the Red Dragon instead of the more customary Union Flag to adorn the memorial to the village's one hundred and twenty-three men and women who served in World War One. Ffynnongroyw's most popular structure, however, is the new and impressive sea wall, replacing the one that collapsed to cause the notorious flooding of 1990.

(MARCH 1992)

FRONGOCH

The University of the I.R.A.

FRONGOCH, a harmless looking hamlet on the Bala-Trawsfynydd road, has earned more than its fair share of notoriety. By 1857 the community was sufficiently established to earn a handsome church, designed by Thomas Mainwaring Penson, famous for Chester's Victorian revival of its now distinctive half-timbered style of building.

But the historic church was demolished nearly two decades ago, leaving only a grassed-over plateau in the graveyard, where a tombstone reminds us that, a long time before Liverpool's controversial Tryweryn reservoir was constructed, two visitors drowned when their boat capsized in the small lake of the same name, further towards Trawsfynydd, in 1880. Five adjacent stones, inscribed only with the name of a local farm (Llaithgwm) and initials DR, JR, TR, AMR and ER conceal some long-forgotten tragedy.

The hamlet's well-stocked shop and Post Office carries the peculiar inscription: 'Home-made house. All bricks and slates produced on Rhiwlas Estate'. This shop was involved in a dispute with Snowdonia National Park authority from 1967 until 1980, when the owner was fined £5 for displaying a tiny sign telling travellers he sold ice-cream.

Frongoch's notoriety began in 1887 during a Sunday morning stroll in Hyde Park, when Liverpool entrepreneur Robert Willis and local landowner R.J. Lloyd Price hit upon the idea of giving Wales its own whisky. Samples of Welsh water were tested and that from Tryweryn was found to be best, resulting in a distillery going into production in 1888, on the site now occupied by the modern Frongoch school. Farmers who were persuaded to provide barley for the new venture made deliveries only in the dead of night, so as not to be seen selling their souls to Bachus.

Armed soldiers had to be used to guard the tax collector's

interests when barrels of the Welsh brew were loaded on special trains at the adjoining Frongoch station. Though now a private house, the rear of of the station looks much the same as when it was built in 1882, still with its original Great Western Railway notices, and a luggage trolley last used in 1961.

The distillery closed in 1900, and in 1915 was converted into a camp for German prisoners-of-war. In 1916 the camp was used to detain eighteen hundred hard-line Irish rebels, arrested after the Easter Monday uprising centred on the Post Office, in Dublin's O'Connell Street. It was on the Post Office steps that James Connolly (later executed) proclaimed the birth of the IRA, but it was at Frongoch, known in Ireland as the University of Revolution, that the IRA was moulded. The embryo IRA evolved and ran the prisoners' lives at Frongoch, where revolutionary lectures, Gaelic lessons, Gaelic games and military drill became part of camp life.

(FEBRUARY 1992)

GLYN CEIRIOG

Pantheon of the good and great

GLYN CEIRIOG Memorial Institute is an amazing pantheon of the good and the great of Welsh history, with a spot reserved for David Hunt, former Secretary of State for Wales, who was born in the village in 1942. It stands in High Street, a seemingly ostentatious name until one recognises the translation of the Welsh original Stryd Ucha, clearly meaning the higher of the village's two streets.

A slate tablet in the garden tells us that the Institute was erected in 1911 as a memorial to poet and station master John 'Ceiriog' Hughes who was born nearby in 1832, and buried in 1887 at Llanwnog, near Caersws, where he looked after the interests of the Cambrian Railway. He represented eisteddfod folk culture at its best, with many of his poems being set to music, the most famous being *Nant-y-mynydd*. A second plaque tells us the Institute was the idea of Mary Davies and fellow members of Glyn Ceiriog branch of the North Wales Women's Temperance Union, and was put into effect by her husband, Alfred Thomas Davies, of Brynhyfryd.

'This Institute was a practical outcome of the Welsh spiritual revival of 1904-05,' says the plaque, which also invites visitors to see the result. After the pious build-up it comes as something of a surprise to find the foyer dedicated to Mammon, adorned with stained glass insignia of 'the seven banking corporations operating in Wales during the Great War 1939-45'. A second glance tells us that even these are now part of history, for they represent, Barclays, Midland, Lloyds, District, Westminster, Martins and National Provincial banks.

Inside one is confronted with more stained glass than the average church, honouring people as diverse as Bishop William Morgan and Colonel William Cornwallis-West, of Rhuthun Castle. The Bishop earned his place by translating the Bible into Welsh in 1588. One suspects the Colonel was honoured for his seven years as MP for Denbigh, but his fame now relies upon the promiscuity of his 16-years-old bride Patsy, a 'friend' of Edward, Prince of Wales, who was believed to be the father of her son George. In 1916 a Sunday newspaper dubbed 63-years-old Patsy Cornwallis-West the wickedest woman in Wales, after an Army court of inquiry into her seduction of a convalescing private soldier, for whom she successfully sought an officer's commission after he had spent a night in her bed at Rhuthun Castle.

One of the many inscribed paintings in the Institute tells us the founder, Sir Alfred T. Davies, 1861-1949, was permanent secretary to the Welsh Department of the Board of Education during 1907-25. David Lloyd George is honoured with both a painting and a sculptured bust. There are busts, too, of such people as the Reverend Lewis Edwards, 1809-1887, Principal of

Bala Theological College; Bodedern-born Liverpool orthopaedic surgeon Hugh Owen Thomas, 1834-91; engineer and inventor Richard Roberts, 1789-1864; and politician Thomas Edward Ellis, 1859-94.

There is a bewildering array of memorabilia, including the witness stand made for the local magistrates' court by convicts of Rhuthun Gaol; there is also a fine chair made by the prisoners. A most unexpected find for those of us accustomed to working in the labyrinthine Houses of Parliament is the original design for the mosaic of St David, which stands high above the entrance corridor to the chamber of the House of Commons, in the Central Lobby.

(NOVEMBER 1991)

GWAENYNOG

Inspiration for Beatrix Potter

GWAENYNOG, an ancient house off the Bylchau road out of Dinbych (Denbigh), has been blessed with some impressive literary associations. With parts dating from the 16th century, it has two 18th century extensions reputedly designed by Samuel Johnson. The house stands at the end of a long drive and when the gardens are open, for part of the year, a notice is placed at the gate informing travellers that Beatrix Potter wrote some of her books there.

The original Gwaenynog was built by the Myddleton family in the reign of Richard III. In later years they were to provide governors for Denbigh castle and MPs for both Denbighshire and Meirionnydd. One of their most famous achievements was to provide water for London, when Sir Hugh Myddleton cut a 38 mile (51km) canal from Ware to Islington. It was opened in 1613 by his brother Sir Thomas Myddleton, who was Lord Mayor of London. Both had become city bankers. Sir Thomas and a fellow Welsh alderman of London, Rowland Heilyn, paid for the printing of the Welsh Bible of 1630.

On 5 August 1774 Dr Johnson visited Gwaenynog with Mr and Mrs Henry Thrale (Hester Thrale, later Mrs Piozzi, daughter of John Salusbury, of Bach-y-graig). He recorded that Gwaenynog was 'a gentleman's house below the second rate, perhaps below the third'. Johnson enjoyed his dinner, apart from the fruit, and noted that after dinner 'the talk was of preserving the Welsh language. I offered them a scheme'. We do not know what Dr. Johnson's scheme might have been, and we had to wait until 1967 for the Welsh Language Act to offer us an alternative scheme, reinforced by another Welsh Language Act in 1993.

Their 1774 host, Colonel John Myddleton, erected an urn-shaped monument to commemorate the visit with the words: 'This spot was often dignified by the presence of Samuel Johnson LL.D.' An additional plaque was added when Johnson died in 1784. Restored and re-sited beside Afon Ystrad in 1975, the monument is accessible to visitors by public footpath across the estate, which the present family bought in 1870.

Dr Johnson was unhappy with the design. 'Mr Myddleton's erection of an urn looks like an intention to bury me,' he wrote to Mrs Thrale, but he did not complain about the inflated inscription. Nearby are the ruins of what is still shown on maps as Dr Johnson's Cottage, though the name is something of a mystery. By 1856 John Williams, author of *Ancient and Modern Denbigh*, was describing the house as Dr Johnson's study, complete with the doctor's chair and table. He claimed eight lines of verse dated 1768, and inscribed on a slate plaque over the front door, were written by Dr Johnson, but this is unlikely. Thought to have vanished some years ago, the damaged plaque is now in one of the outhouses of Gwaenynog farm, where it was shown to me by Major Tom Smith.

His wife, Mrs Janie Wynne Smith, is descended from Fred Burton who bought the estate from the Myddletons, and who was an uncle of Beatrix Potter. Miss Potter spent at least thirteen long holidays at Gwaenynog, where the potting shed is unmistakable in one of her water-colours for *The Tale of Flopsy Bunnies*, whose character Mr McGregor looks suspiciously like photographs of Fred Burton. Beatrix Potter also appears to have used a Gwaenynog cat for *The Pie and the Patty-pan*, according to a letter to her publisher. Beatrix Potter's unfinished manuscript for *Llewelyn's Well*, is inscribed: 'Made and part-written at Gwaenynog, Denbigh.' It was probably written in 1911-12, and contains a description of the Gwaenynog gardens, which have been recently restored.

(JANUARY 1994)

HALKYN

Happily divided

HALKYN is two quite separate communities, and that is without mentioning Pentre Halkyn, a mile (1.6km) down the road. Just to add to the stranger's confusion, one half of Halkyn calls the other half Catch. The Board of Celtic Studies would have us use the perceived Welsh version of Helygain, which purists say should be Helygen, meaning 'a willow tree', but Canon Ellis Davies offered a more plausible source in his 1959 study of Flintshire place names.

He said it was an Old English/Germanic name derived either from *halig* meaning 'holy', or *halga/halgena*, meaning 'saint/saints', and he reminded us of Alken Church, which at various times was written Halking Church, in Llan-saint in Caerfyrddin. There are parishes called Llanfihangel Helygen and Llanfair Tref Helygen in mid Wales. Catch is an easier name to track down for it is a reminder of Halkyn's lead mining days and once referred to a community which grew around a catch whimsey, a horizontal surface wheel used for hand-powered haulage from a vertical shaft.

I began my exploration of Halkyn over an enjoyable lunch at the ancient Britannia Inn, from where one can survey a panorama stretching from Blackpool Tower to Beeston Castle, with Liverpool's twin cathedrals set against the backdrop of the Pennines. It is a truly magnificent view on a clear day. The licensee told me he could trace his predecessors back to 1750, adding that the inn was much older than that, being the last of Halkyn's four inns. This statement ignores the existence of the Blue Bell at the opposite end of Halkyn – but then, that is what the first lot calls Catch.

The Britannia was once part of a small agricultural estate that was sold to the Duke of Westminster in 1807. The Grosvenor family soon stamped their identity on Halkyn. The distinctive lintels on the inn and neighbouring buildings date from their renovation by the Grosvenor estate, but spot the clever concrete copies on a modern extension to the Britannia.

A more assertive W, for Westminster, appears on the facade of the elegant former church school built by the Grosvenors in 1849, with a wing bearing the inscription: 'Enlarged 1898-9, Halkyn Estate'. Most prominent of the Grosvenor additions is the rather fine parish church built at their expense in 1877, the date being preserved on the downspouts. The architect was the ubiquitous John Douglas, of Chester.

The site of the original church can still be identified in the old churchyard, on the opposite side of one of the new roads built by the Grosvenors, enabling them to close the old coach road from Holywell, rendered obsolete by the laying of the A55 in the 1820s. The Old Police Station, in old Halkyn, one can understand. Likewise the Old Rectory, on the road to Pentre Halkyn. Somewhat unusual is the Old Telephone Exchange, in new Halkyn, or Catch. This is a small building dating from the 1920s, which has been converted into a granny flat for the neighbouring house.

(AUGUST 1991)

117

HAWARDEN

Home of Gladstone

HAWARDEN is best known as the home of William Ewart Gladstone, whose posthumous presence is everywhere, but it was already well known during the Domesday survey of 1086, when it was listed as Haordine. This came from two Old English words probably meaning 'high enclosure'. The meaning of its Welsh name, Penarlâg, is just as uncertain, but is also thought to refer to the high ground, this time for cattle, but it might also be of a local chieftain.

Gladstone married Catherine Glynne at Hawarden parish church in 1839, simultaneously with the marriage of sister Mary Glynne to Lord Lyttelton. From 1852 the Gladstones made their home at Hawarden Castle, sharing it with Catherine's brother, Sir Stephen Glynne. Now bypassed, though intersected by a popular commuter rat-run, Hawarden is a delightful place to explore on foot. It has a good car park and a variety of hostelries offering sustenance.

Ecclesiastically, the agriculturally rich Peculiar of Hawarden only came to belong to Wales midway through the 19th century. Although surrounded by the diocese of St Asaph, it was administered from the 10th century by Chester's St Werburgh abbey, and passed into the hands of the absent Lord of the Manor in 1258.

St. Deiniol established its first church in the 6th century. Parts of its 13th century replacement are incorporated in the present mixture of Victorian restorations, mostly Sir Gilbert Scott's work after a fire in 1857. It contains a memorial chapel for Mr and Mrs Gladstone, but they were buried in Westminster Abbey. A gate through the churchyard wall leads to the Old Rectory, which ceased to house the incumbent in 1925. It was used for some years as a college for mature candidates for ordination, and now houses Flintshire Record Office.

Beyond the opposite end of the churchyard stands St Deiniol's Library, a fine building whose purpose is described in its two foundation stones. One, laid in 1899, tells us it was erected by a grateful nation to house Gladstone's personal library, 'for the advancement of divine learning'. The other, laid in 1906, commemorates the addition of a residential wing by Gladstone's eight sons and daughters. An enclosure within the Library garden, but with its own public entrance from Gladstone Way, contains a magnificent bronze and stone memorial to Gladstone, commissioned for Dublin in 1910. By the time it was completed in 1923 it was refused by a Dublin which had become the capital of a new republic struggling to find peace. It was erected at Hawarden in 1925, complete with its figure of Erin.

The pharmacy and adjoining houses, opposite the memorial, mark the site of the thatched cottage home of village carrier Mrs Kidd, and her granddaughter Emmy Lyon, better-known as Lady Hamilton, Lord Nelson's mistress Emma.

Hawarden castle, now the home of Sir William Gladstone, takes its name from the ruins of a Norman castle in the back garden. The estate was sequestered from the Earl of Derby after the Civil War, and sold in 1653 to John Glynne, sergeant-at-law. An older dwelling forms the core of the present house built in 1809-10, with subsequent extensions, including Gladstone's 'Temple of Peace' built in 1887-88 to house his papers. The entrance porch was added in 1889 to mark Mr & Mrs Gladstone's golden wedding anniversary.

What a pity the community never got around to building a statue of Emma Hamilton to leaven the Gladstonian bread for tourism.

(NOVEMBER 1992)

HOLYHEAD

Ireland's gateway

HOLYHEAD creek enjoyed a few decades of naval glory as the fortified western extremity of the Roman Empire, but slipped into a millennium of peace and quiet until 1579, when Queen Elizabeth I placed a barque there for the occasional conveyance of State papers to Dublin. The Irish ferry has been maintained ever since, with minor interruptions due to war, politics or commercial intrigue, but Holyhead has never blossomed into much more than a depot for travellers who want to be somewhere else.

A £380,000 pedestrianisation scheme completed in 1993 enables one to take a leisurely stroll up Market Street for a fresh look at the run-down commercial hub of the town. It starts at the site of the Eagle and Child (beside the war memorial), which was once the terminus for the two-day London-Holyhead mail coach journey. Part of the 1770 hostelry survives as offices, still displaying the solicitor's plate of former Labour MP Lord Cledwyn of Penrhos, Secretary of State for Wales, and later Leader of the Opposition in the House of Lords. Another plaque tells us it was the surgery home of brothers John Fox Russell, VC, MC, of the Royal Army Medical Corps, and Henry Fox Russell, MC, of the RAF, both of whom were killed in World War 1.

More obscure is the inscription on a door lintel at the opposite end of the street, recording that the corner building was erected in 1894 by John Moreton Pritchard, Barrister and JP, who has passed into oblivion. Across the road is the entrance, through the Roman wall, into the graveyard of St Cybi's church. On the left is Capel Llan-y-Gwyddel, part of an early 14th century church rebuilt in 1748 to house the town's first school, and restored in 1980. The ancient church of St Cybi, who gave Holyhead its Welsh name, Caergybi, can be admired only from the outside. Celtic hagiographers tell us Cybi's mother was Gwen, sister of Non the mother of St David. He built his church in 550 AD within the abandoned Roman fort.

A Welsh inscription on the wall of a chapel added to the south side of the chancel in 1897 implies that it had something to do with Queen Victoria's diamond jubilee. In fact it was built as a memorial to local MP William Owen Stanley, of Penrhos. The Stanley chapel window, which cannot be appreciated from the outside, was designed by Sir Edward Burne-Jones in one of his famous partnerships with William Morris.

The Stanley family gave its name to the Port Stanley capital of the Falkland Islands, and to Stanley market, village, fort and prison on Hong Kong island, two areas I happen to know rather well. The 1982 invaders of the peaceful Falkland Islands tried to obliterate Foreign Secretary Stanley's name by renaming the capital Puerto Argentina.

The Chinese have had more lasting success in Hong Kong, where the name of Stanley was changed to Wong Ma-Kok when the former colony was handed back to China in 1997. Until then, the British Army commanding officer's house at Stanley Fort was known as Caernarvon House.

Holyhead churchyard offers the best views of the harbour, now with a new joint ship and train terminal opened in 1991 by Lord Cledwyn, on the site of the old Station Hotel. The forecourt clock, commemorating the Prince of Wales's opening of the previous station improvements in 1880, has been moved from its original platform site.

(SEPTEMBER 1992)

HOLYWELL

An old banking centre

HOLYWELL is a town where pedestrianisation of the High Street has worked reasonably well for the user, with easy access from surrounding unobtrusive car parks, but there is little evidence of consequential commercial affluence.

Prominently located in the street, the former King's Head hotel is now flats. The Victoria Hotel, across the road, survives at its commanding position, looking down the street. In 1862, when it was called the King's Arms posting house, there were plans to demolish the Victoria to make way for a combined market hall and Town Hall. After two years of talk the project was abandoned.

In 1878 the Duke of Westminster laid the foundation stone for a market hall behind the present Town Hall, midway along the High Street. The Town Hall followed in 1896, to serve the new Holywell Urban District Council, which survived until the 1974 reorganisation of local government. One of the inscriptions on the Town Hall (which is now a shop) tells us the clock commemorates the coming of age, in 1867, of Pyers Mostyn, of the Talacre (Roman Catholic) branch of this famous old family. Public subscription paid for the clock, which was originally housed in a stone tower in the street. That tower was taken apart and reassembled, with a few embellishments, in its present position on top of the new Town Hall. The name of the old urban council is preserved on memorial plaques added to the façade after World War One.

Attracted by a sign saying 'This way to a better smile', at the corner of Panton Place, I found it led to the surgery of an enterprising dentist, who proclaims 'Everybody welcome', which is a rare invitation these days. The bonus was seeing Panton Place, and its plaque telling us the houses were built in 1816 by Paul Panton, Under Sheriff of Flintshire, for professional and trades people who worked from home. In 1970 the fourteen houses were converted into fifty-six flats for elderly people, who thus have the benefit of ready access to the town centre a few yards one way, or to a pleasant park a few yards in the opposite direction.

Holywell was once famous for the bank of John Douglas and Christopher Smalley, who went into partnership in 1790 to provide money for the local cotton industry. They opened their banks at Holywell and Mold in 1820, with profits from the Tŷ Gwyn copper mine at Llandudno. Their building still stands, at 20 High Street, but is now a frozen food store. It was taken over by the North and South Wales Bank in 1839, but when that bank was absorbed by the Midland Bank the latter took over the White Horse Inn, to establish the present HSBC premises, whose interior preserves the banking ambience of another era.

Most of the buildings in High Street appear to date from the beginning of the 19th century, some with remarkable continuity, like the pharmacy at No. 35, which was providing the same service in 1835, when it was known as Medical Hall.

(JUNE 1994)

LLANDDOGED

Born out of adultery

ONE could spend a lifetime in the Conwy Valley without ever having cause to visit Llanddoged, a tiny parish amid a network of narrow lanes on a hillside above Llanrwst, where vacant corners of land are now being filled with new houses.

During the 19th century Ffynnon Doged *(Well)*, a short distance north of the church, was reputed to have eye healing properties, but St Doged's identity is lost in the tangled web of half-truths surrounding Wales's early holy men. One tradition says he was the son of a 6th century chieftain named Cedig; another that he was Doeg, son of Prince Maelgwn Gwynedd, and victim of Cedig. Both traditions merge in the belief that the original parish church was built as a martyrium over the grave of Doged, or Doeg, who was slain by a rival for his wife's attentions.

Presumably rebuilt in medieval times, it was doubled in size after the Reformation, by the addition of a parallel nave. The present twin-naved church has an inscribed stone over the southern porch telling us it was rebuilt in 1839 by the Rector, the Reverend Thomas Davies. He and his Eglwysbach colleague, the Reverend David Owen, did most of the work themselves, to create an interior the like of which I have never seen other than in the earliest nonconformist chapels. The focal point is not the altar but the remarkable two-tier pulpit, with its back to the centre of the north wall, rising immediately above the cleric's desk. All three positions are illuminated by a small round skylight in the roof.

There are two painted panels behind the pulpit. One depicts a preacher with an open Bible, beneath the words: *Pregethwch yr Efengyl* (Preach the Gospel); the other is an heraldic hotchpotch, inscribed: *Anrhydeddwch y Brenhin*. That would appear to mean 'Honour the King', but the misspelling suggests that the artist meant to say 'Honour the Queen', for Victoria had come to the throne two years earlier. He simply ran out of space to say Brenhines. He tried to paint the familiar Royal Arms of the Hanoverian period, which incorporated the escutcheon of the Arch-Treasurer of the Holy Roman Empire, but no sovereign ever had a device quite like this – least of all Queen Victoria, whose VR cipher is also worked into the design.

Above the painted boards is a cherub's head, a plaster copy of a marble carving on an 18th century memorial on the east wall, commemorating Sir Thomas Kyffin, of Maenan, who 'joined a most humane benevolent heart to a mind richly gifted by nature, and improved with several branches of polite literature'. There is another ornate memorial to Sir Thomas's father, also named Thomas, 'Attorney General of the counties of Anglesey, Caernarvon and Merioneth, to Queen Anne, King

George I and his present Majesty King George II'.

High-sided box pews, including a well upholstered 12-seater reserved for the Plasmadoc family, are arranged to face the pulpit. The austere iron lectern, with brass desk, was a 1977 gift from local children, to mark the 150th anniversary of their school, though not of the ugly utilitarian part of the building. The village letter box still has its enamelled VR plate.

(JANUARY 1991)

LLANDUDNO JUNCTION

Modern Medieval relic

LLANDUDNO JUNCTION occasionally aspires to a better name than the one that came with its first railway station, built in 1858 to serve the Llandudno branch line – to the everlasting confusion of railway travellers. Before that it was known by the equally utilitarian name of Ferry Farm, though in medieval times it seems to have been called Penlasog. The farm was a refreshment stop for London-Dublin travellers. Its facilities became redundant with the 1826 opening of Telford's suspension bridge into Conwy, and the farmhouse was demolished in 1900.

Ferry Farm Road helps us to locate the hostelry, which stood on the site of the distinctive rounded building designed at the end of the 1920s as a regional showroom for the North Wales Power Company. A few yards around the corner is the North Wales HQ of Trinity-Mirror Newspapers, visited by Prince Charles in December 2000 to open the new Welsh office of the *Daily Post*, which was founded in Liverpool in 1855 as Britain's first penny newspaper.

Traces of the ferry route can be found in the cul-de-sac at the northern end of Railway Cottages, which back on to Glanymor Road. Behind the disguising sheet of painted timber there is an old gate of carriageway width, with a pedestrian wishing gate beside it. The gate preserved a hazardous right of way across the railway lines to the redundant slipway on the other side of the track. Part of a Royal ferry dating from the 13th century, that public slipway was removed to make way for the chasm which now takes the A55 expressway down into Conwy tunnel, opened in 1991. However, a replacement slipway was built into the tunnel scheme, on the river side of the expressway, together with a permanently locked gate to prevent its use, thus presenting posterity with a modern medieval relic.

Members of the Royal family have been visiting Llandudno Junction for seven hundred years, though the first official visit was in 1880, when the future Edward VII arrived by train to turn on the water supply from Llyn Dulyn to Llandudno. Quite unofficial was the visit of Princess Margaret, on a cold January day in 1966. She had been attending the funeral of her father-in-law, Ronald Armstrong Jones, at Colwyn Bay crematorium, and slipped into the Station Hotel to use the lavatory, while on her way to the family home at Bontnewydd, near Caernarfon. By the afternoon some wag had pinned a notice on the door of the Ladies saying: 'By appointment to HRH The Princess Margaret'.

The Station Hotel's most famous resident was Lord Woolton, during his World War II years as Government minister in charge of food rationing, which was administered for the whole country from a multitude of requisitioned schools, hotels, halls and boarding houses at Colwyn Bay. Recently changed to 'Old Station Hotel', it takes its name from the new railway station across the road, built in 1897 to replace the original Llandudno Junction. The 1858 station was opposite what is now a busy Arriva bus depot, which Crosville acquired in 1931 from Royal Blue Buses. Before the building of the 1968 flyover and roundabout, to replace the 1858 level crossing, Victoria Drive came down to the bus depot. Somewhere beneath the roundabout is the site of a 1966 murder, when a 24-

years-old nurse was stabbed by a complete stranger, after alighting from a bus.

(MARCH 1992)

LLANDYRNOG

Abode of the 'Welsh Not'

LLANDYRNOG is one of the few places where the Falkland Islands war of 1982 is commemorated on a village war memorial. Guardsman Peter Edwards was one of the victims of the bombing of the RFA *Sir Galahad*, at Fitzroy. His name was added to the neat and dignified memorial erected in 1919, to honour the 19 young men who died in 'the war to end all wars'. The war memorial stands in the busy churchyard, which is intersected by much-used footpaths, and flanked by two pubs, the Golden Lion and the White Horse, with two thriving grocery shops, an off-licence, a Post Office, newsagent and a butcher across the road.

For such a small community one can only be saddened by the many military tragedies recorded in the church, beginning in 1860 with the death at sea of Captain Richard Edmund Williams, of the 17th Foot (later the Royal Leicestershire Regiment). His home was at Pentre Mawr, built at the start of the 19th century, and still a prominent farm in this agricultural heartland whose economy is now dominated by a big cheese factory.

The village's most elegant house is Glan-y-wern, dating from 1813. It was once occupied by Colonel Philip Stapleton Humberston, MP for Chester 1859-65. One of the parish church plaques tells of the deaths of two brothers from Glan-y-wern in separate accidents in 1928: Gwyn Madocks, 28, of the Coldstream Guards, while flying at Brooklands, and Kenrick Madocks, 22, of the RAF, while motoring in France. Their father, Lt-Colonel Henry John Madocks, was killed commanding the 9th Battalion Royal Welch Fusiliers, at Loos, in 1915.

John Madocks, of Glan-y-wern, is named on the side of the former Baptist chapel as the donor of the land on which it was built in 1836. It is now a smart private house, appropriately named Tŷ Capel Isa, which would appear to be saying 'lower chapel house'. In fact the name, coupled with the little river roaring its way into a hidden culvert on the opposite side of the road, reminds us of the former existence of a water mill, Felin Isa – implying there was once a second 'upper mill.'

Llandyrnog's Wesleyan chapel has also been converted into a house. So has the old church school built in 1834, and one of the authentic examples of the Victorian use of the 'Welsh Not'. The inspector who visited the school in 1847, as part of the infamous Commission of Inquiry into Welsh Education, reported: 'My attention was attracted to a piece of wood, suspended by a string around a boy's neck, and on which were the words WELSH STICK. This, I was told, was a stigma for speaking Welsh, but his only alternative was to say nothing. He did not understand English'.

(JANUARY 1992)

LLANELIAN

The cursing well

NOT quite within the grasp of Colwyn Bay's urban sprawl, the ancient village of Llanelian still manages to maintain its rural identity. Its original name, recorded as long ago as 1291, was Bodlennyn, and its church is dedicated to St Hilary *(Santes Eleri)*, yet its name centres upon St Elian, and for all the wrong reasons.

Tradition has it that having taken ill while walking just

north of the present village, St Elian prayed for water, and a spring appeared. In gratitude Elian prayed that henceforth this well might be the means of granting the wishes of any who asked in faith. But man may wish for good or evil, and Ffynnon Elian came to be known the length and breadth of Wales as a very efficacious cursing well.

Having visited the well in 1773, Thomas Pennant recorded that he had himself been threatened with a curse. The ritual involved writing the name of the person to be cursed on a piece of slate, lead or a pebble. The person buying the curse stood with this in his hand, beside the well while the 'priest' read passages from the Scriptures, and took up a small quantity of water. Some of this was drunk by the 'curser' and the remainder tossed over the sorcerer's shoulder. The ritual was repeated three times while the person desiring the curse muttered his imprecations. At the end of the ceremony the marked object was thrown into the well.

By 1818 the local sorcerer was charging a shilling for a curse, and ten shillings for removing it, and was jailed for a year at Mold assizes, for obtaining money by false pretences. The well was said to be worth £300 a year in fees. There were similar prosecutions in 1820 and 1823, and the Rector destroyed the well in 1829, although the site was used for cursing as recently as 1871, and is still shown on the Ordnance Survey.

The village centrepiece is its church, restored in 1859. It comprises two parallel naves, one medieval, the other more recent – note the different styles in the two east windows. That on the south nave is in memory of John Wynn, of Coed Coch, who died in 1862; that on the north nave in memory of his wife Mary (co-heiress of John Holland), who died in 1844. The crosses were added to the gable ends in 1931. Tombstone inscriptions date from 1587 and include several of the Holland family, beginning in 1612 with Humphrey, son of Pyers Holland, founder of Kinmel.

To reach the church one has to walk across the neat little

courtyard of the White Lion Inn, which is very old, though probably some nine hundred years younger than claimed on one of its walls! Its most famous licensee was John Parry, the bard, who was born at the nearby Y Wern, in 1770. His best known poem was *Myfyrdod Mewn Mynment*, likened to a Welsh equivalent of Thomas Grey's *Elegy written in a country churchyard*. He was buried in Llanelian churchyard in 1820.

On the opposite side of the courtyard there is a store room for the inn, in a well-built adaptation of the old school, built in 1865 by John Lloyd Wynn, of Coed Coch, and endowed in perpetuity with the £154 proceeds of a bazaar held at Coed Coch, and invested in Delhi Railway 5% stock! Just off the square, across the road from the White Lion, Llan farm (once known as Hen Siop) still has its thatched roof. Some of its internal walls (under the stairs) are of wattle and daub construction.

The influence of the Coed Coch estate (into which the Hollands married) is to be seen in the many date stones bearing the initials 'CC', though the Wynns sold the freeholds relatively recently to pay death duties. Many people remember when the then Coed Coch landlord, Miss Margaret 'Daisy' Brodrick and her agent used to visit the White Lion every six months, to collect the rents from her tenants. The estate sold the inn in 1965.

(DECEMBER 1990)

LLANFAIR TALHAEARN

Hymns and bombs

LLANFAIR TALHAEARN, nestling beneath a low hill on the right bank of Afon Elwy, is considerably older than it looks, and very interesting for those who care to look around them. But most travellers bypass it, on the Abergele-Llanrwst road, without cause to cross the bridge leading straight into the centre of the village, between the Black Lion (where I had a pleasant lunch) and the former National School of 1836.

Another hostelry, the Swan Inn, hides behind the Black Lion at the heart of an attractive village square. At the Swan, one half-expects to see the ghost of some teetotal Nonconformist elder of yesteryear, for the seats are recycled chapel pews.

The three-arch bridge has more than architectural interest. It was built in about 1830, when local poet John Jones was a 20-years-old apprentice architect with county bridge superintendent Thomas Penson. He must have had some involvement with its construction, before moving on to greater things, working for Sir Joseph Paxton in the creation of Crystal Palace to house the Great Exhibition of 1851. His later clients included Baron Rothschild, yet locally he is remembered not for his architecture but for his poetry, under the bardic name of Talhaiarn, the minor disparity in spelling belonging to the Welsh orthography of the period.

He took early retirement from architecture, seemingly because of ill-health, and returned to his birthplace, the Harp Inn, which is now a private house known as Hafod y Gân. Its façade has a plaque depicting the profile of Talhaiarn. The inn's mounting steps, which once enabled customers to remount their horses, were removed in a recent controversial bit of land clearance.

This man of many talents shot himself in 1870 but took several days to die, and a verdict of accidental death was returned at his inquest. He was buried close to the door of the parish church, opposite his house, where his grave is marked by a marble obelisk, also adorned with his profile.

The church has its roots in the 6th century, when the Monmouthshire saint Talhaearn, author of the current Gorsedd prayer, settled down as a hermit on this spot. A few late medieval features survive but most of the church dates from 1876. Beside the font at the rear of the church, a hollow sound underfoot reminds us of a covered bath beneath the carpet, once used for baptism by total immersion, in Eastern Orthodox and Celtic fashion.

Wherever one looks there are monuments spanning three hundred years of the Wynne family from Garthewin, an estate including a modern Georgian style house, hidden in the trees on the opposite side of the river. The last of the family's men, R.O.F. Wynne, a prominent Welsh Nationalist, was a Roman Catholic. He died in 1993, leaving three daughters.

Mr Wynne achieved notoriety in 1936 when he stood bail for Saunders Lewis, a founder of Plaid Cymru, while he was awaiting trial for arson at RAF Penrhos, near Pwllheli. In 1977 R.O.F. Wynne told me the petrol and syringes for the arson attack were stored in the theatre he had created at Garthewin, in a converted barn. In 1963 he stood bail for a man charged with causing an explosion at Liverpool Corporation's Tryweryn dam site.

(OCTOBER 1993)

LLANFAIRFECHAN

Before the resort

LLANFAIRFECHAN is divided by the old A55 road (which has recently been bypassed by the A55 Expressway) into the post-1860 resort area on the seaward side and the much older village to the east. Turning off at the traffic lights, into village road, one sees an imposing direction sign, let into the wall, pointing the traveller to the Town Hall, Post Office, Library and Police Station. This is a reminder of the community's grander days, when it boasted of its own urban district council, which vanished in the 1974 reorganisation of local government.

Strangers can be forgiven any confusion on finding the old Post Office permanently closed. The letter box is still emptied and a few yards up the street there is a new Post Office. The library is still there, but with restricted opening hours, and one does not know what to make of the Police Station, which closed in the mid-1990s when North Wales Police abandoned its once-ubiquitous crime-inhibiting presence to concentrate on a few centralised urban stations.

A lane beside the Police Station leads to a most unexpected vista – an entire estate of unmistakable North and Padmore houses. Architect and author Herbert Luck North lived most of his life in Llanfairfechan, where he died in 1941, aged 70. He went into partnership with Percival Mitchell Padmore, who practised until 1972, dying some two decades later. A pioneer in what one might regard as mid-1920s architecture, H.L. North began developing his estate in 1910. He used the thicker rustic slates for his roofs, and always in what the trade describes as diminishing random courses, a skill now lost to all but a few roofing specialists. Much older farm buildings, between this attractive estate and the matching Church Institute, obviously came under the influence of H.L. North for they were also re-roofed at some stage in diminishing random courses, but using the more traditional thinner pure Welsh slates.

Near the old Police Station there is a bridge bearing an 1819 date stone, but there is some confusion as to the name of the river running beneath it. On the village map it is shown as Afon Llanfairfechan but David Roberts, whom I found sitting on the parapet, said he had always known it as Afon Ddu, while others called it Afon Mali. Pointing to the 1862 Llanfair Arms, on the left bank, Mr Roberts said: 'When old Mr Padmore was alive you could time your watch by his lunch time visits to the pub.'

Across the road to the pub, a shop making the flamboyant claim to be 'The original fish and chip shop' was the village's first Post Office, in the early Victorian days when this was the main road between Aber and Penmaenmawr. Also on the bridge, which is a convenient meeting place despite the dreadful hazards of two-way traffic, I met Arthur Morgan, famous in the village as the stonemason with a good memory who was recently brought out of retirement to tell the experts where all the town's troublesome drains were buried.

(SEPTEMBER 1993)

LLANFAIR PWLLGWYNGYLL

Den of practical jokers

LLANFAIR PWLLGWYNGYLL has been the victim of many wicked jokes, but none so bad as the new name boards at the railway station where the trouble started. For two years after the 1848 opening of the Chester-Holyhead railway there was a gap across the Menai Strait, while the Britannia tubular bridge was being built. Passengers disgorged on the mainland to be taken by horse-carriages across Telford's suspension bridge to Llanfair Pwllgwyngyll.

The long wait for everyone to assemble created a captive market for local entrepreneurs who sold refreshments and bogus culture to gullible English and Irish travellers, amused at being marooned in a foreign land. Best known of the Llanfair Pwllgwyngyll inventions is the tall Welsh hat, which was here given its exaggerated length for the amusement of travellers, and rapidly adopted for the same purpose throughout Wales.

Strangers found Llanfair Pwllgwyngyll impossible to pronounce, causing some local wag to extend it by adding the name of the Cardiganshire village of Llandysiliogogo and a lot more besides, to create a monstrosity which is usually reduced to Llanfair PG, derived from the correct name.

After 153 years of lucrative marketing, the whole world is now familiar with the elongated phoney, to which an ill-advised British Rail, some ten years ago, added the unnecessary, insulting and unpronounceable: Llan-vire-poollguin-gill-go-ger-u-queern-drob-ooll-llandus-ilio-gogo-goch, supposedly designed to help pronounce the more traditional version!

As for the station building, I am reminded of an incident in November 1865, when Hedworth Lee, the famous North Wales district engineer of the London & North Western Railway Company, received an urgent message telling him Llanfair Pwllgwyngyll station was on fire. 'Good! Let it burn,' was his reply, for by then it was notorious as the worst station between London and Holyhead. The fire provided the excuse for building the present Station House in 1866. It remained in use until closed in the Beeching cuts a century later.

A more famous fire, in 1970, resulted in the station's being reopened to fulfil its original role. Young boys using paper torches to look for bats inside Britannia bridge set fire to a 120-year accumulation of paint, cable insulation, wooden boxing and oil drips, to generate heat so intense that the famous iron tubes sagged beyond repair. Once again the Chester-Holyhead railway ended on the shores of the Menai Strait and passengers were ferried by bus to resume their rail journey from Llanfair Pwllgwyngyll. As with the original, the new bridge took two years to build, after which the station was again closed.

The platforms were reopened in May 1973 but Station House remained a boarded up eyesore until 1994, when it was refurbished by James Pringle Weavers, who have established a major shop and cafe on the station forecourt, where one can still buy platform tickets bearing the elongated Llanfairpwllgwyngyllgogerychwyrndrobwllllantysiliogogo-goch, which roughly translates as: 'Enclosure of the church dedicated to St. Mary in the hollow of white hazel near a rapid whirlpool and the enclosure of St Tysilio near the red cave.'

A summer house in the garden of Y Graig, near the Toll House, is famous as the place where the European branch of the Women's Institute (originally a Canadian movement) was founded in 1915, at a meeting convened by Colonel Richard Stapleton-Cotton, of Llwyn Onn. Reminiscing in 1975, Mrs Olwen Pierce, the last of the founders present sixty years earlier, told me: 'The movement would also have died at Llanfair P.G. but for Dorothy Drage, of Criccieth, and Alice Williams, of Castell Deudraeth. They were the ones who really spread the WI message in Britain.'

(OCTOBER 1993)

LLANFOR

Tomb built by a horse!

LLANFOR, a tiny Welsh-speaking community hidden away just a couple of hundred yards off the Bala-Corwen road, never built itself a chapel. But it always had a church until October 1991, a date carved in the local memory. It retains a working smithy though no horse has been shod there for about forty years, and the blacksmith's skills are now devoted to repairing farm machinery, or making gates. There is no longer a shop of any kind, and the two pubs have been closed for longer than anyone can remember.

The last incumbent of the parish, the Reverend George Davys Jones, fondly remembered for forty-five years service to the community, retired and moved away in 1969, and was never replaced. Visiting clergy maintained services at Llanfor until 1991 when the congregation of eight was told the church was being closed because of the need for major repairs.

Nothing much to look at from the outside, the present church was built in 1875, and is probably the worst creation of

Benjamin Ferrey, revered elsewhere as the favourite Victorian architect of the Williams-Wynn family. Its interior retains features of earlier structures, including an inscribed stone from the first church, telling us in coded initials that it was built in 1599 by Cadwaladr Prys of Rhiwlas.

The Prices, who were favoured with land after raising a regiment to fight at Bosworth for Henry VII, still live at Rhiwlas. A roadside archway marks the start of a drive up to the house. The first was built in 1574, and much was retained when Rhiwlas was reconstructed in 1809. It was demolished in 1951 but some of its inscribed beams are incorporated in the new Rhiwlas, designed by Sir Clough Williams-Ellis, of Portmeirion fame.

Tombs and memorials spanning several generations of the Prices are to be found inside the church, but the most famous is the churchyard mausoleum inscribed over its locked door: 'As to my latter end I go, to win my jubilee, I bless the good horse Bendigo, who built this tomb for me. Richard John Lloyd Price, 1887.' Bendigo was a profitable race horse and R.J. Lloyd Price was able to admire his tomb for thirty-six years, not dying until 1923. He was the author of many interesting titles, such as *Rabbits for profit, and rabbits for powder*. He also wrote a book about dogs and is credited with staging the first sheep-dog trials in 1873, although the idea probably came from his Scottish shepherd James Thomson.

One of the many interesting tombstones in the churchyard is that of John Williams, a pensioner of the Royal Welch Fusiliers, who died in 1864, aged 87, having survived twenty-seven battles, ranging from Martinique to Waterloo. A plaque inside the church records that the Colours of the Merioneth Militia, raised by the Prices in 1814 [sic], were moved from there in 1980 to the Royal Welch Fusiliers' Regimental Museum, in the Queen's Tower of Caernarfon Castle.

Merioneth Militia's traditions continue in the the 1st Battalion Parachute Regiment. The Merioneth Militia went through several changes of title from 1804, becoming the 7th Battalion Royal Welch Fusiliers in 1908. In the 1939 doubling of the Territorial Army 7th RWF raised the 10th (Merioneth & Montgomery) Battalion RWF. This battalion was disbanded in 1942 when twenty-five officers and five hundred and twenty-seven other ranks volunteered for the new Parachute Regiment, to create 6th (Royal Welch) Parachute Battalion, later merged with the 4th Battalion to make the present-day 1st Para.

(JANUARY 1992)

LLANGEFNI

The Anglesey gallery

ORIEL YNYS MÔN is a superb introduction to the heritage of Anglesey, for those who happen to stumble across it. Opened by the Queen in October 1991, the £1.5m interpretive centre was conceived as a £3.6m art gallery for the three hundred and thirty-three working drawings of wildlife painter Charles Tunnicliffe, which the island's council bought in 1981.

But the project fell foul of parochial politics, and only a tiny fraction of the superb Tunnicliffe collection is on display, within a broader Ynys Môn story. Although intended to be financed by passing holidaymakers travelling across the island, local politics dictated that it be hidden away on a country lane near Llangefni (home of Ynys Môn Council), away from the main tourist route. To find it, follow signs to 'Oriel Ynys Môn', which give no hint of the interesting hour or so awaiting the non-Welsh-speaking explorer (except Mondays, when the centre is closed).

The sophisticated tableaux, spanning 2,000 years of history, are well captioned. Here, for instance, one can stand at the door of an ancient burial chamber and marvel at its construction. One can enjoy such diversions as a visit to the well of St Dwynwen, Wales's patron saint of lovers who is our equivalent of St Valentine. Having solved her own love problems with prayer, Dwynwen founded a small church on Llanddwyn island, to where countless lovers have taken their problems ever since, some to consummate their love in the church ruins.

Another complicated story set in Anglesey is that of Branwen, who became Queen of Ireland, but was demoted and put to work in the court kitchen. Using a friendly bird, she summoned her brother Bendigeidfran to her rescue. In the ensuing war Ireland was laid to waste by the Welsh, Branwen's jealous half-brother Efnisien murdered her son, and Bendigeidfran was mortally wounded. Branwen returned to Ynys Môn to die of a broken heart, and was buried near Llanddeusant.

A Celtic slave chain reminds us of discoveries made during World War Two, when peat was scooped out of Llyn Cerrig Bach to cover the sand which was ruining the engines of fighter aircraft at RAF Valley. With the peat came the most significant hoard of Celtic treasures ever found in Wales.

Charles Tunnicliffe is given just a small corner of Oriel Ynys Môn, in which there is an inspired reproduction of his studio window, and the view beyond to Malltraeth. From time to time some of the travelling exhibition space is used for extended displays of Tunnicliffe's work. He illustrated more than a hundred books during the course of forty-five years, mostly from his Malltraeth home, but some people never forgave him for having been born in Cheshire.

(MAY 1992)

LLANGERNYW

5,000 years old yew tree

LLANGERNYW has the benefit of brown and white boundary signs which indicate a major tourist venue – something not readily apparent to the casual visitor. A misleading clue is to be found on a roadside plaque, seen when approaching from Abergele, inscribed: 'Sir Henry Jones cottage ¼ mile.' It sends strangers down a lane to a farm that has nothing to do with the cobbler's apprentice who was to be knighted in 1912 for his services to education. Sir Henry's home, which was bought for the nation in 1934, is at quite the opposite end of the village!

The village centre is small and compact, around the T-junction with the road to Llansannan. Its tiny population has one general store which is also the Post Office. Across the road is the old public fountain.

Now refaced in slate, the fountain has its original plaque, inscribed: 'Whosoever will let him take of the water of life freely. 1860.' Residents can remember it as the general water source, which they were forbidden to use on Sundays. The old smithy is recognisable behind the fountain; so, too, is the elegant house labelled Tŷ'r Gof, which tells us that this was where the blacksmith used to live.

Despite the suggestion that Llangernyw is a tourist centre, the interesting looking Stag Hotel, advertising its accommodation, bar meals and traditional ales, was well and truly shut when I called. The same was true of the Bridge Inn, with its advertisement for good food, where the licensee told me they only opened in the evenings and on Sundays. 'What we would take in the day wouldn't pay for the electric light,' he said of this would-be tourist honeypot.

There used to be five livestock fairs a year at Llangernyw, with an overspill into the churchyard where, in 1749, the porch of St Digain's was said to be used as a place where butchers hung and sold their meat. In October 1995 the Tree Council

140

declared the yew tree in the churchyard to be five thousand years old, the oldest and biggest in Wales and England, although there is an older one at Fortingall, Tayside in Scotland. Of ancient origin, the present church is a mixture of medieval and Victorian work. It contains some interesting monuments, especially to several generations of owners of Hafodunos, the parish's finest house. Though difficult to read, the oldest inscription I could find related to Roger Lloyd, who died in 1610.

In 1831 Hafodunos was bought by Liverpool shipowner Samuel Sandbach, who is duly honoured with a marble stone recording his death 20 years later, aged 81. Recorded, too, is the death of his grandson Major Henry Sandbach, at Aden, in 1895 'from wounds received while lion hunting in Somaliland'. Hafodunos had become an old people's home, until the magistrates closed it in September 1993. After that there was an abortive controversial proposal for converting it into a luxury hotel for homosexuals – a development that might have justified those brown and white tourist signs.

A plaque in the church records the death in 1923 of Thomas Gee, son of the famous Denbigh printer, 'while shooting near Llyn Gwythlyn', aged 75. In addition to the church there is Bethabara Baptist chapel, with a date stone of 1830, and the Presbyterian Capel y Cwm of 1836, rebuilt in 1909.

At the entrance to Glanrafon farm there is a 'sunburst' gate, removed from the early 19th century turnpike toll house nearby, and identical to the gates introduced by Telford for his improvements to the A5 road in 1815.

(NOVEMBER 1993)

LLANNERCH-Y-MEDD

Town of 250 cobblers

LLANNERCH-Y-MEDD used to be one of the biggest market centres in North Wales, resulting in what is now more of a small town than a big village, with ample evidence of its past glory. The community grew around the T-junction of the roads from Holyhead, Amlwch and Llangefni, and straddles Afon Alaw, which is now culverted and out of sight. It became the natural commercial centre for northern Ynys Môn.

Centrally located at the junction is the parish church, with a massive tower of medieval proportions, though it is an 18th century rebuild on older foundations. The tower is surmounted on the east side by an architecturally incongruous bell-cote. The bell-cote is copied on the over-sized lychgate, which has a date stone of 1755, and through which one enters a graveyard of distinctive Caernarfonshire slate headstones. The church porch was devoid of the customary notices and I was unable to find anyone who knew where the key might be available for an exploration of the interior, which has a 14th century font.

Vying for prominence with the church is the adjacent public convenience block, also built in medieval proportions though a relatively modern structure adorned with a beautifully gilded bilingual notice carved on a slab of Meirionnydd slate. Its heavy iron gates were locked, and obviously had been for a very long time judging by the mound of wind blown debris on the other side, though it used to be the pride and joy of Twrcelyn Rural District Council, subsumed in the 1974 reorganisation of local government.

The former council office, a conversion of the old Poor Law workhouse, carried a 'For sale' notice, as did so many other buildings, including once thriving shops at the very hub of the town. A plaque records that land for the school, which used to serve the complete age range, was given in 1858 by William Roberts. Three chapels, Baptist, Presbyterian and Independent, all of classic Nonconformist simplicity, still serve the community.

In 1833 the town boasted two hundred and fifty cobblers and clogmakers. It was also a manufacturing centre for snuff, made from tobacco imported at Amlwch. When these industries were linked to the local cattle market Llannerch-y-medd was also a town of taverns, of which only two survive – the Bull and the Twrcelyn Arms.

Matching its commercial importance, Llannerch-y-medd was once an important printing centre, and it was a pleasant surprise to find the fascia board of 'Jane and Elizabeth Jones, Printing Office' still in situ. They were in business from 1877 to 1890, but their printing shop was founded in 1864 by Lewis Jones, and is still printing. No relation to the founders, John Hywel Jones, 62, whom I met on site, was the third generation of the present family of printers. He and his sister, Mrs Eurlys Williams, 73, were born on the premises. During recent changes in the yard they found an 18 ft (5m) deep well containing pure water, and the remains of a horse driven milk churn.

(DECEMBER 1993)

LLANRWST

Hong Kong of Medieval Wales

LLANRWST once debated the practicalities of applying for membership of the United Nations – its residents having long derived smug satisfaction from the phrase: 'Cymru, Lloegr a Llanrwst' *(Wales, England and Llanrwst)*. The saying possibly stems from the periods 1247-55 or 1277-82, when Afon Conwy was the treaty boundary between English armies and the kingdom of Gwynedd, with Llanrwst caught in a lawless No Man's Land in the middle. When the colonial castle towns were built by Edward I, the penal laws – the most 'racial laws in the history of the world' – excluded the Welsh from holding any land, tavern, house or shop in them. The Welsh were prohibited to hold a market even within 10 miles of such a privileged colony. Llanrwst lies 11 miles from Conwy and over the years developed as a significant market town. In the 18th century, it was the 8th largest town in Wales.

Few would recognise that among today's shuttered shops, in a town whose residents believe the decline began in 1964, when the Town Hall was demolished for no obvious benefit. It was an early 19th century building in the town square, with market hall at ground level and assembly hall above, incorporating the bell, date stone and clock from the original market hall of 1661.

The demolition was the work of Llanrwst Urban Council whose name survives – appropriately enough – only on the gates of the cemetery in Nebo Road. One of the few responsibilities of its successor, Llanrwst Community Council, is to look after its rich inheritance of footpaths, but when did the councillors last try to negotiate what used to be a delightful river walk, beneath the churchyard?

Having lost its commercial ethos, Llanrwst should capitalise on its very considerable tourist potential at the heart of Llywelyn ap Iorwerth's (the Great) favourite territory. The medieval link is preserved in the parish church of St Grwst, the last resting place of Llywelyn's ornate stone coffin. Initially buried in his abbey at Conwy, Llywelyn was moved in 1284 to make way for the parish church of Edward I's new borough. Edward gave the monks land for a new abbey, upstream at Maenan, where the coffin rested until the Tudor dissolution of the monasteries in 1536. From there it was rescued by the ubiquitous Wynn family, of whom Sir Richard, treasurer to Queen Henrietta Maria (consort of Charles I) built the Gwydir Chapel in 1634, as a distant annex to St Grwst's church. There the empty coffin now rests, beside the intricately carved and fully inscribed coffin lid of Hywel Coetmor ap Gruffydd Fychan ap Dafydd Gam, believed to be the illegitimate son of

Prince Dafydd, and from whom the Wynns derived their estates.

One could spend an hour just studying the monuments in the Gwydir Chapel, but even more magnificent is the choral gallery and rood screen in the main body of the church. A rare example of medieval carved oak, this too is said to come from Maenan Abbey, to where it was taken from the original Conwy Abbey.

Everything one sees from the churchyard is pure 17th century, including the row of twelve former alms houses whose future has been debated for a couple of decades. It is now eighteen years since Aberconwy Council agreed to their use as a craft museum, but why not convert them into three or four delightful houses?

The town's most obvious architectural feature is its humpbacked bridge across Afon Conwy. It has three arches, the middle one being some 60 ft (18m) above the average river level. Its parapets contains the Royal arms and date 1636, and the structure is commonly attributed to Inigo Jones. He could have had something to do with the design, but it is doubtful whether he ever visited the town.

Tu Hwnt i'r Bont is an early 17th century house on the left bank, famous for its Welsh teas in the summer months. The road past the house leads to the much-restored Gwydir Castle, of which little more than the shell relates to the home of the Wynns.

(AUGUST 1992)

LLANSILIN

Where Glyndŵr worshipped

LLANSILIN church is where Owain Glyndŵr would have worshipped, and where he may have been baptised after his birth at nearby Sycharth, on an unknown date around 1354. Sycharth was Owain's favourite estate despite the implications of his appended second name, derived from family lands at Glyndyfrdwy. Internal pillars of that ancient church, with their ornate capitals, still survive in the present building, along with extensions of the 15th and 16th centuries, including a balcony once needed to cope with all the worshippers.

Bullet holes in the ancient south door date from the Civil War, when Parliamentary troops stormed the church on 23 February 1646, to use it as a stable. Many of the church's artefacts were destroyed by the troops, including an ancient statue of its heavenly founding patron, St Silin. A fairly modern uninscribed box tomb in the churchyard is today pointed out to visitors as St Silin's grave! It is, in fact, the grave of the Reverend David Richards, vicar of Llansilin during 1819-27, and who was also known as Dewi Silin.

The churchyard's yew trees are calculated to be about 1,000 years old. The most poignant of the gravestones records the deaths in 1892 of the wife and six children of Edward Williams, Ty Coch, Sychtyn: Annie, 5, on March 16; Charles, 2, on the 21st; Sarah, 10, on the 23rd; Mrs Williams, on the 24th; Mary, 8, on the 28th; Rose, 8, on the 30th; and David, 6, on April 4; all victims of a diphtheria epidemic.

Beside the south wall is the grave of Huw Morris, the prolific poet Eos Ceiriog, who died in 1709, aged 87. An upright stone restores what George Borrow was unable to read when he visited Llansilin in 1854.

'Taking off my hat I went down on my knees and kissed the cold slab covering the cold remains of the mighty Huw,' wrote Borrow, adding that the only legible part of the inscription was

'1709'. Twenty-one years after Borrow's visit a three-light stained glass window was installed in the church in memory of Huw Morris.

An enormous 24-candle brass chandelier was added to the chancel in 1824, with a chain and pulleys to a wall-mounted cranking handle, enabling it still to be lowered and raised when needed. Borrow never saw the chandelier or any of the church furnishings. The pub landlord who guided him through the churchyard did not know where to locate the key – a frustrating problem I have often encountered on my travels.

He never named the pub. Only the Wynnstay Arms remains licensed, but there used to be four more: Old White Lion, The Hand, Butcher's Arms, and Traveller's Rest. There are still four chapels, belonging to the Baptists, Wesleyan Methodists, Congregationalists, and Presbyterians.

There is a modern school, in a superb location. Inside is preserved the bell from the original school of 1878; the clock appears to be from the same source, with time now standing still at 10.41. The old school is now a private house, with a commemorative stained glass window appropriately inscribed 'Hen Ysgol,' and still preserving the roadside plaque of its 1878 opening by Mrs Hanmer, of Glan-yr-afon.

(AUGUST 1994)

LLANYNYS

Scarcely a hamlet, but good food

LLANYNYS is scarcely big enough to be described as a hamlet, yet it has one of the most interesting churches in the whole of Wales – if you can find it, down some of the narrowest lanes in Dyffryn Clwyd. Its name and topographical evidence suggest the founders chose a rare dry spot in the old marshland between the rivers Clwyd and Clywedog, in an area once too wet for a village to develop.

As with many old churches, it acquired an adjacent refreshment house, the Cerrigllwydion Arms, which I found to be surprisingly busy with people who had sought it out for lunch. Taking its name from its founder, 18th century attorney Edward Edwards, of Cerrigllwydion Hall, the pub was built on the site of church stables where worshippers would once have placed their horses, while preparing for the afternoon service. There may well have been an earlier ale house on the same site but the present pub was built early in the 19th century, when Edward Edwards was allowed to set it back into the churchyard so as to avoid obstructing the view of Denbigh castle from the Vicarage, which was built in 1808. Now a private house, the large and handsome brick Vicarage has become obscured from the pub by trees. It stands in fine gardens at the end of a short drive whose gateway is beside that into the churchyard.

Also in this hub of the community are the mounting steps (which once served horse riders attending either the church or the pub), a Victorian letterbox and one of Sir Giles Gilbert Scott's original Jubilee telephone kiosks with 1936 crown. Apart from two houses almost hidden behind church, and pub, and a modern bungalow a short distance away (where one might borrow the church key) there is nothing else in Llanynys.

St Saeran's church is a double-naved building, with a double bell-cote on the southern half, bearing a 1684 date stone and housing two contemporaneous bells. The gate leads to the west face, in which one can again see the original 13th century doorway into the northern nave, uncovered in the 1960s when an outer coating of plaster was removed from the church walls. The present entrance is through a porch on the southern side, and a door dating from about 1490, on which are carved inscriptions and the dates 1544, 1598 and 1602.

On entering the church one is confronted by a large 15th century coloured mural of St Christopher, found in 1967 during the removal of countless layers of whitewash. Beneath it stands the reconstructed tomb of a 13th century Bishop of Bangor who retired to the obscurity of Llanynys because he could not endorse the government of Llywelyn ap Iorwerth. Old pews, with their inscriptions and dates, were reused long ago to create the choir stalls and for panelling the chancel, in which the altar, a simple carved table, was the gift of Colonel William Salusbury, who defended Denbigh castle for King Charles in the Civil War.

(SEPTEMBER 1993)

LLANYSTUMDWY

Den of the Welsh Wizard

LLANYSTUMDWY has renewed its place in history as a political shrine, with the 1990 reopening of the much-enlarged Lloyd George Museum. Fortuitously, the new A497 by-pass enables us to stroll through the village in much the same way as the young David Lloyd George would have done.

He was born at Manchester in 1863, but when 17 months old his schoolmaster father died, and his mother was given refuge with her unmarried brother, Richard Lloyd, the Llanystumdwy shoemaker. Uncle Lloyd's modest home (incongruously named Highgate), and adjoining workshop, are now part of the Lloyd George shrine and the starting point for the tour of the very compact village. It is easily recognisable from the older bilingual plate which informs us it was Lloyd George's home until 1880, and a more recent gaudy addition, in the form of a big inauthentic sign portraying a boot and the words: 'Richard Lloyd, gwneuthurwr' which Lloyd George would not have recognised.

Just a few steps away are the outstanding gates to the museum which, with an impressive array of exhibits, a reconstructed classroom, speeches from a 'talking head', and archival film screened in a small video theatre, spans the life of the man dubbed the Welsh Wizard.

A short walk through the museum grounds leads to another pair of gates, adorned with the elephant and castle Royal badge, although in this case taken from the seal of the old borough of Pwllheli, which donated the gates in 1952. On the opposite side of a rural lane (leading to the house where Lloyd George died in 1945) is his lonely grave. It stands in a locked enclosure on the wooded banks of Afon Dwyfor, where he often sat, both in youth and maturity. Thick with brown winter leaves when I last saw it, the tomb was designed by Sir Clough Williams-Ellis.

The riverside path immediately below the tomb is a public right of way, but beware of following it downstream of the village bridge, where it is littered with such environmentally friendly signs as: 'Land and fishing strictly private', or 'Members only start here', and the excruciating 'Cricc'th & Ll'ystumdwy AA Waters'.

This was the bridge Lloyd George would cross to and from the village's church school. Someone is the proud possessor of an oil painting of it executed by my father, for the 1979 National Eisteddfod, at Caernarfon. Nearby are the ruins of the 1866 Moriah Presbyterian chapel, which was burnt down in 1935. It was replaced a year later by the present Moriah, opposite the museum – another example of Sir Clough Williams-Ellis's architecture. That was where Lloyd George worshipped in the eventide of his life, although he had been brought up in a minority Baptist sect. Tiny Tabernacl chapel, set back from the village street and opened by the Congregationalists in 1831, closed in 1990.

Before leaving Llanystumdwy cast a glance at the village Institute, built in 1912 with the proceeds of a libel action arising out of Lloyd George's complex love life.

(JANUARY 1991)

LLECHWEDD VILLAGE

Old pennies for new

PENTRE LLECHWEDD is a make-believe village of yesteryear, where beer costs about fourpence-three-farthings a pint at the Miners' Arms, and a good lunch can be bought for about a shilling. It is a place where children can still buy a penn'orth of boiled sweets at the corner shop of Angharad Ellis, or a farthing postcard at Crimea House. Harp music drifts across the square from the cottage of David Francis, whose bardic name, Y Telynor Dall o Feirion said everything, for he was the blind harpist of Meirionnydd. He died there in 1929, having been born in the same bed 64 years earlier.

The journey into the yesteryear of Llechwedd begins at the Old Bank, with an exchange of modern money for re-minted Victorian coins. It is found in one of the surface buildings of the tiny community which grew on the fringe of Llechwedd Slate Caverns, at Blaenau Ffestiniog. Its last resident moved out in the 1970s, as train rides into the Victorian caverns became a prize-winning honeypot, attracting such visitors as Princess Margaret, the Crown Prince Naruhito of Japan, and the Duchess of Gloucester.

Take the path between the two rides to find the almost hidden entrance to Llechwedd Village. Opposite the Smithy is the Old Bank bearing the name Greenway & Greaves, a partnership that survived until 1887. Now a museum, the Old Bank still displays 'today's exchange rate', starting with a farthing for 10p, and ranging through the ha'penny, old penny, three-penny bit and sixpence, all of which can be used in the village. The reverse of each coin is authentic, apart from modern dates, but the sovereign's head is replaced by a locomotive adorned with the double-headed eagle of the Greaves family.

In 1846, while seeking the blue-grey slate which was to provide roofs for every continent, John Whitehead Greaves lived in the ancient cottage later made famous by David Francis. It was then the only house in the bleak roadless pass, built with round boulders gathered off the mountainside long before man found the slate blocks that have since shaped everything else.

Next door to the 'Bank' is the village lockup, where you can peep through a cell window which, like the cell door, formed part of Betws-y-coed Police Station from 1872 to 1970. As well as enhancing the make-believe village, the lockup serves as offices for the security man, who patrols in Victorian policeman's uniform.

An 1887 letterbox, made by Handyside & Co, is still in use on the village square, outside the exciting Victorian sweet shop at Crimea House, a name which reminds us that the Crimea Pass section of the A470 road, linking Meirionnydd and Dyffryn Conwy, was opened during the war of 1854. The shop is adorned with a carving of a Royal Welch Fusilier in the scarlet tunic of the period.

Until the centralisation of all North Wales postmarking at Chester, visitors could despatch post cards with special letter railway stamps at Llechwedd village, for re-posting deep underground in the adjoining Llechwedd Slate Caverns. Some of these, commemorating special events, such as the centenary of the Conwy Valley Railway, or royal visits, have become rare collectors' items.

One of Giles Gilbert Scott's 1936 telephone kiosks – the famous Jubilee K6 – also adorns one side of the village square, with an old AA kiosk on the other side.

(JULY 1991)

LOGGERHEADS

Where Mendelssohn strolled

LOGGERHEADS, some three miles (5km) south-west of Mold, preserves the memory of an old boundary dispute between Denbighshire and Flintshire – which were briefly amalgamated within the county of Clwyd from 1974 to 1996. Grosvenor family greed, for royalties on lead ore lying hidden in these parts, caused a thirty-year dispute which the family lost in an Exchequer Court decision of 1763. The court ruling was carved into a tablet, set into what looks like a stone sentry box still standing beside the A494 road. Though no longer readable, the tablet recorded that a boulder in an arched recess at the base had long been known as 'Carreg carn march Arthur' (that is, the stone of the hoofprint of Arthur's horse), and marked the medieval boundary. The argument had by then caused the 17th century travellers' inn, still standing on the opposite side of the road, to be known as The Loggerheads – then a common description of dunces or blockheads.

This was where Richard Wilson, founder-librarian of the Royal Academy, used to do his drinking, after he inherited Colomendy, behind the inn, in 1781. He settled one of his drinking bills by painting an inn sign inscribed 'We three loggerheads', and depicting two pipe-smoking men standing back-to-back, the third loggerhead being the viewer. Wilson's original board is now preserved behind glass, inside the inn, but the modern replacement is a close copy. A year later he crossed the road (a hazardous operation these days!) to stroll beside Afon Alyn, in what is now the Loggerheads country park, and there he collapsed and died, aged 69, his dog running back to the inn for help.

Another famous customer of The Three Loggerheads was Felix Mendelssohn, who stayed there in 1829, when he was inspired to compose one of his lesser-known piano pieces after following in Wilson's footsteps along the banks of Afon Alyn.

Now we can all share that path, and a lot more, thanks to the founders of Crosville Motor Services, who turned up at the 1926 auction of the Loggerheads Estate. Crosville was one of Britain's biggest and best equipped bus services, dominating the territory from Cheshire to Lampeter.

Brothers Claude and Jim Crosland-Taylor had set out to buy the inn, to which they were already running lucrative bus trips from Birkenhead, but the price went too high. Instead they bought 74 acres across the road for £1,600, and built the rival Crosville Tea Garden, which became a popular excursion venue until World War Two. Clwyd County Council bought it in 1974 for conversion into the present country park – with free admission.

The car park, information centre, cafe, shops, and working water mill which still produces flour, have been added to a 1½ mile (2.4km) walk along the river bank, and up to the top of the cliffs, all of which make a good cheap day out. The path is either a nature trail or an industrial trail, depending upon which map and guide one buys at the outset. One is marked with observation points of geological or botanical features, or the great variety of birds which live here. The other map pinpoints mellowed remains of the lead mining industry which once flourished here – long enough ago for nature to have reclaimed old man-made scars.

(JULY 1991)

MAENTWROG

Where Nonconformity was hidden

MAENTWROG means 'Twrog's stone', which is a symmetrically rounded glacial boulder of enormous proportions standing upright outside the west wall of the parish church. Indentations at the top are said to be the handprint of St Twrog, a 6th century Breton holy man who threw it from the 2,334 ft (710m) summit of Moelwyn Bach, some three miles (5km) away! Maen Twrog smashed the altar of a pagan community whose existence is said to be demonstrated in the churchyard, for the evergreen yew was a pagan symbol of immortality.

The first recorded evidence of the Christianity which St Twrog brought to these parts is in an archiepiscopal return of 1504, when Maentwrog is described as a chapelry of Ffestiniog. The most famous Rector of the then single parish was Edmwnd Prys, during 1572-1624. He took up residence at Tyddyn Du, Gellilydan, after he had been appointed Archdeacon of Meirionnydd in 1576, and played a prominent role in Bishop Morgan's translation of the Bible into Welsh. He was also absentee Rector of Llandudno, whose tithe income he enjoyed.

Though reputed to have been buried beneath the altar of Maentwrog church, none of that building seems to have survived within the replacement of 1814, by which time the village plan was much as we see it today. Robust and well-designed buildings, all made of course slate stone, formed part of the Tanybwlch Estate until about three decades ago, and remain a remarkably cohesive whole.

Tanybwlch is the big but less architecturally inspired house on the opposite side of the river, from whose windows you will see no hint of Nonconformist worship in Maentwrog. When allowing the Methodists to build a chapel in the high street the landlord stipulated that its rear, facing Tanybwlch, should be disguised to look like a private house (which is what it has since become).

Much of the story of the Tanybwlch family may be gleaned from memorials in the church, which was embellished and extended by the estate in 1896, to designs by famous Chester architect John Douglas. By that time the estate had passed, through marriage, into the hands of Blaenau Ffestiniog quarry owner William Oakeley (1828-1912), described on his memorial as 'a very great gentleman and a fine sportsman . . . beloved by everyone'. His wife Mary did all the superb wood carvings in the church.

The high street lych gate, also by John Douglas, was erected by the Estate in 1897, to mark the diamond jubilee of Queen Victoria, and is very unusual in that it incorporates a clock.

Now dedicated to St Twrog, the pre-1896 church honoured St Mary, whose name is still preserved in St Mary's Well, which can be found by taking the stone steps opposite the Post Office and village store. Alas, the well, which was never made into an architectural feature, is now much neglected and half-hidden in dumped garden refuse – with even worse fly tipping a little higher up – so out of keeping with the general appearance of the village.

(MARCH 1991)

MOELFRE

On the Royal Charter trail

LITTLE remains of old Moelfre, apart from its pattern of narrow streets clinging to the cliffs of eastern Ynys Môn. The once humble cottages of its founding fishermen and quarrymen have been modernised, nearly all by the addition of an upper storey.

Moelfre's maritime traditions are now proudly concentrated on its lifeboat house, extended fourteen years ago to accommodate the 25-ton *Robert and Violet*, which incorporates all the latest rescue technology.

'Many people have tried to identify Robert and Violet, but with no success,' said full-time lifeboat mechanic Tom Jones, when I called at the house. The 47ft boat, costing £600,000, was donated anonymously to the RNLI on condition it was stationed at Moelfre. 'The donor obviously had local links but we have no idea who it could have been,' said Mr Jones.

From the lifeboat station, built in 1909, one can see the distant roof of the original boat house of 1848, since when ten Moelfre lifeboats have rescued fifteen hundred lives. Missing from the impressive record boards, which line the interior walls, is any reference to Moelfre's most famous shipwreck, the *Royal Charter*, in which four hundred and forty-four people were drowned on their way to Liverpool from the Australian gold field.

It is a silent reminder that the storm on that dreadful night, in October 1859, was too violent to allow the launch of the village's six-oar boat, but any visit to Moelfre inevitably becomes something of a *Royal Charter* trail.

Having parked near the Post Office, to walk into the network of cul-de-sacs, you can take the footpath along the top of the cliff to the site of the wreck. It takes about twenty minutes to reach the cliff-top memorial erected in 1935, although the path is muddy in wet weather, and boots are needed to cross the narrow intervening bog. From the memorial one can see both the rocky shelf a little to the north, on which the Liverpool steam clipper was wrecked, and the shingle beach from which many more than the lucky 39 would have been saved if she had drifted a few hundred yards to the south. Her twisted iron ribs can still be seen at very low tides, and there are those who still dive in the hope of recovering some of her missing gold, said to be worth £3m.

Up the road, in Llanallgo churchyard, where one hundred and forty of the victims were buried, there is an obelisk memorial recording much of the tragedy at the end of a two-month voyage. It tells us the victims were buried by the Reverend Stephen Roose Hughes (whose family name lives on in North Wales), and that another forty-five were buried at Penrhos Llugwy, by his brother Hugh. Others lie buried in churchyards as far away as Llandudno.

The signal gun from the *Royal Charter* stands outside the old Llanallgo Rectory (now a private house) next-door to the church. This was where Charles Dickens stayed with Roose Hughes when reporting the disaster for his weekly magazine, later reprinting the episode in *The Uncommercial Traveller*.

(MAY 1991)

MOEL-Y-DON

A famous ferry

MOEL-Y-DON still has its stone jetty, to remind us of its days as a ferry point for crossing the Menai Strait to and from what has been known at different times as Llanfair-is-gaer, Aber Pwll, Port Dinorwig and Y Felinheli.

Diarists who recorded their crossings included John Wesley, both in 1750 and 1756, on his way to preach Methodism to the Irish, though the nearest he got to spelling Moel-y-don was 'Baldon'. On the second occasion he slept the night before at Caernarfon. Next morning he rode his horse for an hour along the shores of the Menai Strait until opposite a house he took to be Moel-y-don. He called across the Strait in vain, and when it began to rain moved on, to find shelter in Llanfair-is-gaer church, where a little girl told him he had to ride a further couple of miles to find the ferry. There he again shouted across the Strait and the ferry 'came over without delay and soon landed us in Anglesey'. Moel-y-don was an ancient Crown ferry until as recently as 1935. It was reopened by the two county councils in 1938 and operated for another decade or so.

The attractive old ferry house still stands, bearing a slate date stone inscribed 1717 and the initials 'BED', set in a triangle which makes it difficult to know where they begin. Two shallow ponds, one overflowing into the other and fed by a spring, occupy what would otherwise be a front garden, but I cannot think what their purpose might have been. Between the house and some old cottages beside the jetty the low tide reveals the interesting skeleton of a sizeable boat, though its name and history have long been forgotten. It appears to have been a Thames sailing barge abandoned in the first half of 20th century. In 1997 it was used as a training base for forty students of the marine archaeology unit at Bangor's University College.

The parish name is Llanedwen, and the tiny community still has its church, where regular services are held. Rebuilt in 1856, the church stands in the middle of fields, to the right of the lane leading up from the ferry. The only other building in the immediate vicinity is at the end of a short drive on the left of the lane. This is a 16th century gem called Plas Coch which, somewhat unexpectedly, I found to be a pub, open to the public though licensed as part of the caravan camp on the estate. Its origins are inscribed in stone over the front door: 'IN THE YERE OF LORD GOD 1569 DH MAD THYS HOU', where the mason ran out of space. When deciphered it tells us David Hughes made Plas Coch.

The house was handed down through the Hughes family until William Bulkeley, of Brynddu, took his daughter to Dublin in 1735. There he introduced her to some excellent claret, *The Beggar's Opera*, and Liverpool privateer Fortunatus Wright, who had captured at least sixteen French ships, and by whom she became pregnant. A hasty marriage was arranged and their resultant daughter Anna eventually married Roger Hughes, of Plas Coch. From this union the estate remained with the Bulkeleys well into the 20th century.

Some distance away, but also within the parish of

Llanedwen, is the better-known Plas Newydd, home of the Marquess of Anglesey, and now in the care of the National Trust.

(NOVEMBER 1993)

MONTGOMERY

Old gateway to Mid Wales

ONCE the gateway to mid Wales, the old county town of Montgomery is today a delightful backwater, oozing civic pride – even the public toilets are equipped with hot water and bars of soap.

Still preserving its medieval plan, the little township lies beneath the fortified outcrop which gave Montgomery its strategic importance, guarding a ford across the Severn (Afon Hafren). The original Montgomery is in Normandy, from whence Roger de Montgomery turned up in 1067 as Earl of Shrewsbury, whose territory came to include a large slice of mid-Wales.

He built the first Montgomery castle, on the site now signposted as Hen Domen. Destroyed by the Prince of Powys in 1095, it was rebuilt and eventually given by Henry I to Baldwin de Boulers, from whom the town derives its Welsh name, Trefaldwyn.

That castle was replaced a mile to the south, by the present post-Civil War ruins, built between 1223-53, during which the town was granted its first charter, in 1227.

As part of the 750th anniversary celebrations countless informative plaques were affixed to buildings to record something of their history, such as the fact that medieval references to the brook which provided the town's sewer, undér Broad Street, name it as Schitebrok!

Broad Street now forms a neat town square, thanks to the removal in 1748 of the central market hall, which was replaced by the present Town Hall at the bottom of the street. The Broad Street frontages were modernised from about 1750, to create a delightful Georgian vista. The half-timbered frontage of the Dragon Hotel, once the coaching inn, is an early 20th century addition.

Many genuine half-timbered buildings remain, notably in Arthur Street where one is used by the local civic society as a museum. This building retains structural elements of its many earlier uses as an inn, bakery, butcher's, post office and general stores. The former Wesleyan Methodist chapel, built in 1863 at the corner of Arthur Street and Princes Street, is now a textile design workshop. The town's other chapel, still used by the Presbyterians, was built in 1885. The foundation stone was laid by David Davies, MP for Cardiganshire, not to be confused with the man of the same name who became MP for Montgomery in 1906. The parish church, dating from the 13th century, deserves a day's exploration all on its own.

A little distance down the hill one arrives at Gaol Road, which is not a reference to the obvious 18th century gaol, still with barred cell window, at the street corner, where it remained in use as a police station well into the 20th century. It was replaced in 1830 by the county gaol, complete with treadmill, hidden by some trees around a bend at the bottom of Gaol Road. On strolling round the trees one cannot help but be surprised by the massive archway, complete with Royal Arms, added in 1866 to impress villains. The gaol is now converted into flats.

(APRIL 1993)

NANNERCH

The Buddicom village

NANNERCH display's a plaque saying it was Clwyd's best kept village of 1987 – which means it was overtaken a long time ago! It is nevertheless an attractive village, with surprisingly wide roads, though now bypassed. Nothing remains of its medieval past, but the earliest surviving reference is in a tax return of 1254, and the spelling has remained constant since 1291.

The first building one sees when entering the village is the half-timbered Station Lodge, bearing the date 1875 and monogram W&MB. It was designed by Chester architect John Douglas for William Buddicom, of Penbedw, engineer for the Mold and Denbigh Junction Railway, which opened in 1869.

In these days of concern about the future of the North Wales coast railway it is strange to think of places like Nannerch once having their own stations. This one was demolished to make way for the more recent bypass road on part of the railway track bed.

William Buddicom died in 1887 but his family name or initials appear all over the village, though not on Tai Cochion, a semi-detached pair of rustic brick houses built to his instructions in 1878, also to the design of John Douglas. Across the road from Tai Cochion the modern village hall has a plaque which simply records, without dates or explanation, the names of William's son Harry, 1859-1925, and grandson, Lieutenant Walter Buddicom, killed in action in 1918, aged 24.

I did not know what to make of the brick-clay Buddicom monograms on the modern extension to the older Ruabon brick village school. One bears the Latin 'AD' but the date has been hacked away for some obscure reason. The Buddicom's three-storey home in Penbedw park was demolished in 1958.

Two houses nearing completion in 1992, in the village centre had already taken their place with the older architecture, having been built with stones salvaged from the demolition of buildings on the smithy yard. By today they could pass for 18th or 19th century structures – but for their concrete window sills.

The rectors of Nannerch can be listed from 1254 but their present church is an unspectacular 1852 design by T.H. Wyatt (constructed at a total cost of £1,314). It contains items taken from the former church, including a memorial to Watkin Williams, an earlier owner of Penbedw, who was the local MP from 1777 to 1806. Other memorabilia of the original Penbedw family, and of the earlier church, include a big chandelier given by Elizabeth Williams in 1820. The Buddicoms are also very well represented with memorials, including a chest given in 1958. One window, on the north side, contains the Royal Arms of around 1500, but the most spectacular adornment is a Grinling Gibbons marble piece of 1694, in memory of Charlotte Mostyn though now used as a display board by the Sunday school.

(JULY 1992)

NANTGLYN

Eccentric lexicographer's haven

NANTGLYN, a remote and once self-sufficient hamlet west of Dinbych, is best known for its eccentric antiquarian and lexicographer William Owen Pughe, who believed Welsh was the language of heaven, from which stemmed all other tongues. In a bid to prove it, he spent eighteen years compiling a dictionary of 100,000 words, including some he invented, to demonstrate a Welsh vocabulary which did not borrow from any other roots, and earned a Cambridge doctorate for his work. (Dr Johnson's English dictionary, as enlarged by Todd, contained 58,000 words).

One might be forgiven for thinking he developed his bizarre

linguistic theories on the banks of Afon Lliwen, a tributary of Afon Clwyd. But his dictionary was already published when, at 47, he arrived at Nantglyn to inherit the name and estate of his uncle, Rice Pughe, Vicar since 1788, whose wife gave the church its silver communion set.

W.O. Pughe was born at Llanfihangel-y-Pennant (Meirionnydd) in 1759, spent his childhood at Egryn (Ardudwy), went to school in Altrincham, and at 17 migrated to London, where he was influenced by the founders of the city's Gwyneddigion, a literary society regarded as the custodians of Welsh traditions.

By the time he was buried in Nantglyn churchyard, in 1835, his name was inscribed as Gwilym Owain o Veirion, using the strange orthography he had devised for his Welsh. Other relatives are buried in the same tomb, built like an altar at the northern edge of the cemetery, where the land falls away sharply to a field and the river. The family dominates the memorials inside St James' church, which was rebuilt in 1777, on foundations recorded 500 years earlier. The east window is in memory of W.O. Pughe and his grandson William Owen (son of Aneurin Owen, only son of W.O. Pughe). The elegantly carved reredos is in memory of Catherine, first wife of Meilir Owen, great-grandson of W.O. Pughe.

A peculiar feature of the ceramic tiles set into the reredos is the inversion of the Greek letter omega (Ω), theological partner to the alpha (A) on the other side. Unfamiliar with the *Book of Revelations*, the local craftsman of 1870 thought it was a horseshoe to be placed in the traditional 'good luck' position. The southern windows commemorate Meilir, erected by his second wife Ellen. The west window is in memory of Jane, wife of Aneurin, erected by her son Meilir. As recently as 1962 a plaque was erected by Churchill Owen and his sister Myfanwy Lloyd, in memory of Ellen Owen.

I was fortunate in being shown the church by Miss Elian Jones, the Rector's Warden, who told me of a rare coincidence in 1940, while she was serving with the Army in Leicestershire. 'There, in South Wigston church, I recognised the east window, for it was exactly the same as the one at Nantglyn, both having been made by O'Connor, in 1861,' she told me.

A pulpit and stone steps have been built within a yew tree of some 30 ft (9.1m) girth in the churchyard. Local tradition says John Wesley preached there. Nearby is the ornate tomb of Robert Davies, the poet and grammarian Bardd Nantglyn, who was born in the hamlet. Also born at Nantglyn, in the Vicarage, was David Samwell, the naval surgeon who was with Captain Cook when he was killed in Hawaii in 1779.

Nantglyn has a school, built in 1859. There is an Independent chapel, and the Presbyterians are not far away. The hamlet has a Post Office, but no shop – and no pub.

(JANUARY 1994)

NEFYN

Chartered by the Black Prince

DESCRIBING Nefyn as a village is guaranteed to upset some of the the inhabitants, who are quick to tell you that Edward, the Black Prince gave them a borough charter which was confirmed by Richard III. The only obvious reminder of their once-municipal status is the inscription on St Mary's Well, in the town centre, stating it was rebuilt in 1868 by Nefyn Corporation, and naming Lord Newborough as Mayor – an office which used to be held for life if you were important enough in these parts.

In one way or another the Wynn family of Boduan and Glynllifon, who became the barons Newborough, were able to meddle with the law to control Nefyn for centuries. Nefyn's first known tourist was King Edward I. He liked the place so much he held his international victory tournament here, after his conquest of Wales in 1284.

Edward's great-grandson, the Black Prince, gave Nefyn to one of his knights, Nigel de Lohareyn, for service at the Battle of Poitiers in 1356. Nefyn was already a well-established centre under the kings of Gwynedd – Owain, the brother of Llywelyn II had his court here. With the royal gift came a charter to establish Nefyn as an English mercantile colony, but no protective castle was ever thought to be necessary here. That ancient mercantile role, never based on anything more than seasonal catches of herrings (5,000 barrels exported in 1747) is still reflected in the presence of a part-time bank (although there were three until five years ago).

Nefyn's character remained Welsh throughout the Middle Ages, supporting Owain Glyndwr's revolt in 1400. However, predatory local gentry had gained control of Nefyn by the end of the 16th century, completing the take-over in 1812 by manipulating the Enclosure legislation to deprive the inhabitants of their 300 acres of common land.

The skyline view of the church tower, with a weathervane in the form of a brig in full sail, is an obvious focal point when approaching Nefyn. On reaching the old church, which was rebuilt in 1827, one finds it is now labelled as the local maritime museum, which I am sure would have been worth a visit if only I had been able to gain admission. Despite a notice saying the museum was open I found that even the churchyard, whose gravestones presumably tell a lot about the town's history, was locked for the winter.

The parish is now served by St David's church, unusual in that it bears only four memorial inscriptions, including an exterior 1903 date-stone beneath the beautiful east window. When viewed from the inside the window reminds us that Nefyn was once on the ancient route for pilgrimages to Ynys Enlli (Bardsey).

Nefyn also has a full complement of Nonconformist chapels, whose influence may account for the fact that the town now has only one public house, *The Sportsman* (1856), compared with the fifteen recorded at the beginning of the 19th century. It also has a smart-looking hotel, the *Nanhoron Arms*, where a pot of tea for two on a cold February day was my bargain of the year.

Before leaving this corner of Nefyn the stranger should mount the steps of what looks like a medieval tower, behind the church. It is a 19th century watch tower, built simply to provide a panoramic view of the bay, the mountains and the intervening strip of land on which Nefyn is built.

(FEBRUARY 1991)

NORTHOP

An orphan's legacy

MANY of us who never had cause to enter Northop, are now compelled to chicane through the narrow and hazardous middle of this surprisingly old village. Lateral thinking, when planning the A55 Expressway, has placed it astride the new link road from North to South Wales. The planners concentrated on east-west travel, and gave little thought to the effect of severing the 1930s bypass, south of Northop, with an expressway to the north.

We usually find ourselves trapped in a fast-moving convoy, and unable to stop, as we snake past one of the most interesting-looking churches in the Welsh border country. It once served a much bigger Llaneurgain parish, from which the younger parishes of Fflint, Connah's Quay, Caerfallwch and part of Rhydymwyn have been hived off. The five-stage tower dates from the late 15th century, as we are reminded by the portcullis and Tudor roses among the royal devices carved (and renewed in 1965) in the stonework surrounding the west door. Construction dragged on through the reigns of Henry VII, Henry VIII, Edward VI, Mary and Philip, and into the time of Elizabeth I.

The rest of the church looks authentically Tudor, but was completely rebuilt in 1839-40, the interior being a John Douglas restoration of 1877, retaining some medieval monuments. In the churchyard there is a fine school building dating from 1609, which was restored in 1975 for European Architectural Heritage Year, and is well worth a peep through the windows. The National School which succeeded it in 1823 still stands in the village, but that, too, was replaced in 1974 by Ysgol Owen Jones.

Presumed to have been born out of wedlock, the infant Owen Jones was found abandoned in the church tower, round about 1600, after the wardens went to investigate the irregular ringing of the eight o'clock curfew bell. He was fostered in the village and eventually apprenticed as a butcher in Chester, an event commemorated in the city with a plaque, on what later became the Midland Bank. Owen Jones bought lots of land from which trustees, appointed under his will of 1658, still use the rents to help educate the children of Northop.

One is surrounded by history when walking through this compact village, many buildings bearing such names as The Old Police Station, The Old Vicarage, The Tannery, Smithy House, etc. Date stones have long been a feature of the village: I spotted 1829 on a building in the High Street, 1841 on what was obviously once a chapel at Fiveways and 1915 on the first extension out of Connah's Quay road, and 1989 on a modern extension of the Red Lion.

What of the date stones of the future? Lots of residents were worried by rival development plans to encircle Northop with two golf courses, a hotel, office block and housing complex on one 247-acre site, and a scheme for replacing a natural bog with a lake and promenade, and houses on the rising meadow beyond. The first scheme was up and running by 1990, leaving the community divided in its opinions.

(OCTOBER 1990)

168

OVERTON-ON-DEE

Alias Flintshire detached

OVERTON-ON-DEE is an elegant village which in 1992 held a great summer celebration for the 700th anniversary of its foundation charter from King Edward I. The village has retained the grand medieval scale of its planning, though most of what we see today is Victorian. It lies at the heart of what was variously known as Flintshire Detached, Maelor Saesneg or English Maelor, an administrative area created by Edward as part of his Earldom of Chester.

Overton parish is a combination of the medieval townships of Overton Villa, Overton Foreign and Knolton, all known in Welsh as Owrtyn Fadog, after a 12th century Prince of Powys who is said to have had his castle here. Not until the 1536 Act of Union (of England and Wales) did it revert to Wales – a legal nicety, seeing that the Earl of Chester had long been a subsidiary title of the Prince of Wales. However it remained in topographical limbo as Flintshire Detached until 1974, when it became part of Wrexham Maelor, within the new county of Clwyd (dissolved in April 1996).

A relic of its independence can be seen on a gable wall of Overton Surgery, in the wide High Street. Built as local council offices in 1956 (and given a Civic Trust Award three years later), it displays a stone carving of a strange Red Dragon with a Satanic face – though I failed to find anyone who had noticed it!

St Mary's parish church sits neatly at right angles to the High Street, entered via a battlemented west tower which sports both a clock and a sundial, the latter dating from 1803. Most of the red Cheshire sandstone church is the work of Victorian restorers, who incorporated earlier parts. The church was seriously damaged by fire in July 1993, when a juvenile was charged with arson. In the churchyard four poles prop up an ancient yew tree which used to be listed as one of the seven wonders of Wales. Not so obvious is the roofless cemetery chapel, hidden in trees off Wrexham Road, and once famous for its stained glass. It was erected in 1860 as a memorial to Anna Maria Peel of Bryn-y-pys.

Chained gates on Wrexham Road remind us this used to be the start of the drive to Bryn-y-pys, which was demolished in 1956. The Lodge bears the date 1875 and monogram of Edmund Peel. A private house across the road has a plaque recording its construction as a cottage hospital in 1905, in memory of Edmund Peel.

Wrexham Road now accommodates a simple Roman Catholic church, built in 1958 as a memorial to local martyr Richard Gwyn, executed at Wrexham in 1584 and beatified at St Peter's, Rome in 1970. Overton is blessed with many useful inscriptions and date stones, like the public fountain erected to mark Queen Victoria's golden jubilee in 1887. Next-door the date 1884 on an iron downspout is the only visible record of when the first Police Station came to Overton.

On the opposite side of Penyllan Street one can read 'Cocoa and Reading Rooms', on an 1890 temperance institution that still serves the community, now as a recreation centre and public library. An interesting-looking footpath at the end of Penyllan Street is disappointing – it leads to the local sewage works.

(FEBRUARY 1992)

PENMAENMAWR

Twixt Paradise and Eden

PENMAENMAWR's stone parapet and granite plinth, inconveniently set in a tiny triangular flower garden, at the top of Paradise Road, look a bit battered but they once again support a bust of the Right Honourable William Ewart

Gladstone, 'Grand Old Man' of Victorian politics – a recent replacement for the original bronze of 1899. For 14 years the little garden did no more than mark the last resting place, so to speak, of the man who served four terms as Prime Minister: 1868-74, 1880-85, 1886, and 1892-94.

Having married Catherine, sister of Sir Stephen Glynne, of Hawarden Castle, in 1839, the Liverpool-born Liberal took up residence with his bankrupt brother-in-law in 1852, and bought the castle in 1867.

For reasons shrouded in mystery, Gladstone made the quarrying town of Penmaenmawr his favourite holiday haunt, staying at several different addresses over a period of many years. Penmaenmawr was but an hour's train ride away from Hawarden, and frequent visits by Mr and Mrs Gladstone gave a boost to local traders who ingeniously created a tourist industry out of the GOM and the alliterative slogan 'Penmaenmawr, the prettiest place in the Principality' – there being no Trade Descriptions Act in those days!

When the GOM died at Hawarden in 1898 the citizens of Penmaenmawr decided he should live on for the benefit of tourism, in the form of a bronze bust looking out to sea from the top of Paradise Road – a road just then acquiring some local notoriety.

Paradise Crescent, at the bottom of the hill, had been built in 1897 against the wishes of some local magnate. He had his revenge by erecting a high building across the road, to blot out the Crescent's view of the coast. He called his monstrous house Coll Gwynfa – which is Welsh for Paradise Lost. But Paradise was made to reign at the top of the hill, in the form of Gladstone's tourist-pulling bust, atop a six-part plinth of local granite which, by 1964, was very much in the way of modern traffic. That was the year Penmaenmawr Urban District Council proposed moving Gladstone from Paradise Road to the garden of Eden Hall, where they had their offices until the 1974 reorganisation of local government.

Whether or not the GOM was tempted by the women of the night he invited to tea at 10 Downing Street, and for whom he built welfare homes in Soho, the people of Penmaenmawr decided it might be tempting fate to commit his ghost to the Garden of Eden, and the argument continued for the next thirteen years.

Satanic forces decided the issue one dark night in 1977 when the bronze bust disappeared. The inscribed plinth remained in the triangular garden while the town debated the merits of finding a replacement bust.

'We think a replacement statue of a quarryman would make more appropriate street decoration than the undignified headless Gladstone,' said the community council chairman in 1979, by way of a reminder of the real economic base of the Prettiest Place in the Principality. That issue was also decided by outside forces, when a car demolished the granite plinth in 1984. The salvaged pieces were reassembled in the Garden of Eden but the triangular parapet remained in Paradise Road. In 1990 the town invested in a replacement head of the Victorian friend of prostitutes, but argued for many months as to where best to unite bust, plinth and parapet. The debate taxed all the diplomatic skills of the opposing Eden and Paradise schools, but Paradise won the day.

(SEPTEMBER 1990)

PENMON

A place of good hope

THE BLEAK seascape of Penmon is a most unlikely place to look for a rich cluster of memorials to fifteen centuries of concern for the rescue of man's body and soul.

The headland's first known resident was St Seiriol, a 6th century hermit. Traces of his stone cell may still be seen beside his well, at the end of a walled causeway across what had become an intervening bog by 1990, when it was restored to a fish pond. Out of Seiriol's cell grew Penmon Priory, recorded in the chronicles of Basingwerk Abbey as having been founded in the 6th century by Maelgwn Gwynedd.

Vikings destroyed the original priory in 971 and it was replaced by the present building during 1120-70, with an eastern extension in the 16th century. In the older ruins you can look upwards to what would have been a second storey, to see the window seat from where a monk would read aloud during otherwise silent meals.

The existing church is behind the priory ruins. It is still in regular use. Its door is usually open, the interior is illuminated and a very useful plan and guide sheet is on sale. It has superb Norman arches and remnants of 12th century arcading. Also such relics as a 10th century stone cross from which one arm was lopped off so it could be used as a window lintel. Also on show is a piece of 13th century Limoges enamelled copper, found five feet (1.5m) below the floor near the old altar. By way of continuity there is a glass case containing the pennant flown by the old Liverpool-Llandudno-Menai Bridge steamer *St Seiriol*, during her seven epic voyages to Dunkirk in 1940, when she rescued twenty thousand British troops.

Nearby is an enormous dovecote, built in the 17th century by the Baron Hill estate, local beneficiaries of the dissolution of the monasteries. I have known it open but it is usually padlocked. Beside the dovecote is the open gateway to a toll road, that is unmanned during the winter, that leads to the spit of land directly opposite Ynys Seiriol/Puffin Island (where both St Seiriol and Maelgwn Gwynedd were buried). For most of the time the only sounds are the wind, sea, seagulls and half-minute tolling of the fog bell on Trwyn Du lighthouse, built in 1837. It was once manned, hence the two sturdy houses built in 1839, whose porches are still adorned with the coat of arms of Trinity House.

Behind the Trinity House cottages are the older cottages of Penmon lifeboat crew who operated from 1832 to 1911. A lane leads to the remains of the lifeboat ramp. The unmistakable old lifeboat house was converted into a very comfortable cliff-top home by Sir Goronwy Owen, a one-time Liberal Chief Whip, who was MP for Caernarfon County during 1923-45.

Lifeboat and lighthouse were a direct consequence of the disaster which befell the Liverpool-Beaumaris paddle steamer *Rothsay Castle*, which sank within sight of Penmon in 1831. The upturned hull that may now be seen at low tide, 350 yards (310m) off shore, is the Hull dredger *Hoveringham III*, which sank in January 1971 after springing a leak off Ynys Seiriol. Four of her crew were taken off by Beaumaris lifeboat, another three staying with the vessel until she began to roll over, when they took to their own lifeboat.

The *Hoveringham III* actually lies off Penmon quarry (not readily visible from this point) which supplied the 'Penmon marble' to make the towers of Menai Suspension Bridge, the best of the Georgian buildings in Beaumaris, and also Birmingham Town Hall.

(DECEMBER 1990)

PENNAL

The Delphi of Wales

UNMENTIONED in most guides to mid Wales, Pennal is a very attractive village, west of Machynlleth. It oozes communal pride in its rich inheritance from its days as the Welsh Delphi, the very centre of the Welsh world.

'Come and relax, share the peace, enjoy our history,' says the invitation to the graveyard encircling the church of St Peter ad Vincula – chains having been welded into the gates to remind us of its meaning: St Peter in Chains. In the churchyard, signposted as Heritage Garden, an explorer might expect to see

Pythia, priestess of the Delphic oracle, waiting for a consultation on one of the seats erected among the tombstones.

Passing the church was once a hazardous operation, but the road was recently widened after residents of all denominations helped move numerous old graves. Reburial within the remainder of the cemetery provided the opportunity to create the Heritage Garden, in which tombstones (mostly from the once busy slate quarries above the village) have been reset in a variety of themes, such as chronological sequence, a collection of village crafts, a display of local carving skills, etc.

The church displays a facsimile of *The Pennal Policy*, which Owain Glyndŵr sent from here to King Charles VI of France in 1406, setting out his conditions for recognising the jurisdiction of the Pope of Avignon (instead of the Pope in Rome). Held to be Wales' most important surviving document, it was borrowed from Paris in 2000, for display at the National Library, Aberystwyth, during the commemoration of the sixth centenary of Glyndŵr's revolt. Glyndŵr sought recognisable symbols of national independence, such as an archbishop for Wales (achieved finally in 1920) with jurisdiction over the bishops of Exeter, Bath, Hereford, Worcester and Lichfield, as well as the Welsh dioceses. He set out the medieval agenda for the struggle to maintain the Welsh national identity, and that is now manifested in the political, linguistic and educational arenas of modern Wales. The document was drafted by the local archdeacon while Glyndŵr's court was ensconced at Cefn Caer – a medieval farm still standing on a Roman site a short walk from the church.

Pennal church was founded in the 6th century by St Tannwg and St Eithrias, and was renamed by the Normans some time before 1120. It was one of nine Meirionnydd churches listed in the Taxatio of 1253, and became an independent parish in 1683. Stones from the Roman fort were used to rebuild the church in 1769. It was again rebuilt in 1810 and finally restored in 1873, retaining the 16th century roof timbers, pulpit and oak pews.

Encircling the churchyard one finds the community's only inn, the school, two shops, public conveniences, a small parking ground and two rival places of worship. A plaque on the Presbyterian church records its foundation in 1869 and reconstruction in 1908. Devoid of name or date, the Congregational chapel now confines its activities to the vestry.

Most village activities take place in the church room, beside a Celtic cross memorial to the dead of World War One, including a soldier awarded the VC. A separate memorial honours the crew of six killed when their Wellington bomber crashed nearby in 1941. In such a neat village it is strange to see the crudely painted prohibitions: 'Private. Dim parcio', daubed either side of the church room.

(AUGUST 1993)

PENRHYN BAY

Port of Prince Madog

PENRHYN BAY was described at a 1969 public inquiry as a place where people tended to reside for about five years. 'Why is that?' asked the Welsh Office inspector, who was investigating a petition against plans for a children's play area to commemorate the Investiture of the Prince of Wales.

'We arrive at sixty-five and depart at three-score-years-and-ten,' said the witness, who was objecting to having his retirement disturbed by the sound of happy children. No one would now recognise that description of a fully balanced community, with a thriving junior school of over one hundred and sixty pupils.

The play area was built and named Prince's Green, on an old sand pit, the remains of ancient wind-blown deposits quarried away by the building trade. Nearer the sea, off Penrhyn Isaf Road, a clay pit, in which houses with big cellars were built about twelve years ago, once supplied the brick trade from a pier of which there is no longer any trace. Another jetty served the Little Orme limestone quarry, opened up in the 1870s when small quarries of an earlier era were already apparent.

By today one has to look very hard for evidence of all this industrial activity around which Penrhyn Bay grew, originally with a few workers' homes (Quarry Cottages, in Maes Gwyn Road) and a more impressive dressed stone house for the manager. Next came the tin houses, small wood and corrugated iron bungalows, one of which survived in Marine Road until 1985, still with oil lamp lighting.

Neighbouring Llandudno on one side, and Colwyn Bay on the other, were still describing the place as The Klondyke as recently as 1921, when Llandudno Road and Penrhyn Hill were opened up to modern traffic.

For all that, Penrhyn Bay has its roots in the earliest annals of Welsh history. Still proudly standing near the foot of Penrhyn Hill is Penrhyn Creuddyn, a house even older than the 1590 date stone over one of its fireplaces. It is better known as Penrhyn Old Hall, and is now used as a pub and licensed restaurant.

In 1987 I was the only British journalist in the Vatican for the beatification of the Venerable William Davies of Penrhyn Creuddyn, born in 1555 at Groes-yn-Eirias (Colwyn Bay), and hanged at Beaumaris castle in 1593, for his treason in preaching Roman Catholicism, and for his subversion in producing the first Welsh book to be printed in Wales – *Y Drych Cristianogawl* (the Christian mirror) – on a press set up in a nearby cave on the sea face of the Little Orme. The beatification service, in the vastness of St Peter's, was historic in a wider context as the first at which the Welsh language was given official Vatican status and used by Pope John Paul II.

Even older than Penrhyn Hall is the sunken garden at Odstone, the lone house on the Rhos-on-Sea and Penrhyn Bay golf course, once the natural outlet of Afon Ganol now diverted and culverted. In 1955 contractors building the present sea wall telephoned me to take a look at a natural extension of the sunken garden. It was a medieval quay wall which their excavations had uncovered. Here was proof of the folk memory of the great days of Rhyd y Cerrig Gwynion (ford of the white stones) as a harbour.

Also known as Aber Cerrig Gwynion this was the harbour from which the man history names as Prince Madog is said to have sailed with two ships in 1170, to discover America 322 years before Columbus, an event commemorated on a modern inscribed plaque on a section of ancient wall in the garden of Odstone. There is a matching plaque on the shores of Mobile, in Alabama, saying that was where Madog landed. Assuming the voyage did take place, the best candidate for the adventurous mariner was Madog Gloddaeth, whose nearby medieval home (Gloddaeth Hall) has gone through many changes to become today's St David's College.

The golf course surrounding Odstone provided the emergency airfield for the first aircraft to land in Wales, in August 1910. It was a Farman, flown by Robert Loraine, who had taken off from Blackpool to make the then longest recorded oversea flight of sixty-three miles. Born in 1876, Robert Loraine was an actor when he joined the Montgomeryshire Yeomanry to serve in the Boer War. He returned to a successful stage career, interspersed with some interesting pioneering flights.

(MAY 1994)

PENTREFELIN

Grave of a Baptist martyr

PENTREFELIN has a name to remind us that three flour mills astride Nant-y-garreg-ddu once made this tiny community an important focal point in the agricultural economy of Dyffryn Conwy. The brook can still turn a two-ton 18ft diameter wheel at Felin Isaf, a name indicating it was the lowest and last in the sequence. This wheel was installed in 1740 in a new building, but the original mill is still operational at the rear, where it was well established as long ago as 1690, when it formed part of the wedding dowry of a local woman.

Felin Isaf was worked until 1942 and reopened in 1979 after Government agencies paid two-thirds of the £80,500 restoration bill. It was sold in 1985 and now attracts 20,000 visitors a year. It is well worth a visit for it is Wales's best-preserved example of a high-tech mill of its day, with some unusual features, like the 1850 oat kiln – the only one ever made in north Wales.

Felin Uchaf *(upper mill)*, which once operated on the other side of the A470 road, is now only a house name. Traces of the third mill can be found in a field some half-a-mile (800m) upstream.

A modern bridge, barely recognisable as such, has taken the A470 Llandudno-Cardiff trunk road across the brook since 1960, but the local bus service still uses the old bridge. Bus operators prefer to call the place Fforddlas, as do all Baptists, who have given the community its only place of worship since 1786. The present chapel was built on the same site in 1841, and I was revisiting it for the first time since 1937, when I was taken to hear the Reverend Lewis Valentine preach, after he had served nine months imprisonment for political arson during the construction of RAF Penrhos, a bombing school near Pwllheli.

A plaque above the door of the adjoining chapel house tells us (in Welsh) that the eminent sculptor John Gibson, RA, was born there in 1789 – which would have been while his Ynys

Môn-born father was a gardener at Marle Hall. One of my favourite cities is Rome, and those who enjoy puzzles should travel to the city where Gibson lived and worked for 48 years, and where the epitaph (written by Lord Lytton) on his ornate white marble tombstone tells us he was born at Conwy on 19 June 1790. Both inscriptions agree he died in January 1866, but the chapel memorial says he was 77, while the dates on the Rome tombstone produce an age of 75. Less obvious is the Rome tombstone, several rows lower down, 'erected by his affectionate brother John Gibson, RA' for Benjamin Gibson, who died in 1851 aged 40.

John Gibson was probably born at Gyffin, Conwy, from where the family moved to Fforddlas in 1791 when the father became a gardener at Bodnod (Bodnant). In 1795 the father, a Baptist preacher, fell out with the deacons at Fforddlas and moved back to Gyffin; moving in 1799 to Liverpool, where Gibson said he had great difficulty speaking English.

Fforddlas cemetery is no less interesting than Rome's famous Protestant Cemetery, access being through a gate leading into a tunnel beneath the chapel vestry. With nearly all the epitaphs carved on slate, the white marble pillar on the grave of the Reverend Robert Roberts is all the more obvious. Look at the Welsh inscription on the back of the column, in memory of Ann Evans, of Bryncariwch, Glanconwy. It tells us she was beaten to death by her husband in 1800, for disobeying him in seeking baptism from the Reverend Robert Roberts.

(SEPTEMBER 1991)

PENRHYN CASTLE

Slaves and munificence

PENRHYN CASTLE revisited was an unexpected lesson in social history, quite unlike what I had experienced in 1952 when reporting its first opening to the public. A newspaper cutting of what I then wrote was distributed to journalists attending the 40th anniversary celebrations in 1992.

In 1952 I obviously felt sorry for Lady Janet Douglas-Pennant who, in giving her 380-room home to the National Trust, in settlement of inheritance tax, said: 'The castle will remain a memorial to my family.' Forty years on I saw the castle as an epic memorial to the Jamaican sugar slaves and the Bethesda quarrymen who had created the wealth with which it was built during 1820-34.

As early as 1845 a visitor recorded that a wander through its incredibly ornate rooms of Norman proportions was 'like struggling along in a bewildered dream'. It took me nearly three hours to wander through the dozen or so rooms that are open to the public.

I was waylaid not so much by the overwhelming magnificence of the stone and wood carver's skill, and the opulence of the furnishings, but by the much smaller exhibits which other visitors were content to pass without so much as a glance.

There was, for instance, the illuminated address presented in 1866 by 'we the quarrymen and other residents of Penrhyn Quarry', congratulating the first Baron Penrhyn on his elevation to his 'so deservedly entitled' peerage. However cynically one may view the document today, it did add: 'We cannot look around without beholding durable evidences of your munificence and judicious liberality in the shape of churches, schools, hospitals, model cottages and numerous other improvements.'

Then there was the 1875 address, set out bilingually in

Welsh and English, by 'workmen in the employ of the Penrhyn family', congratulating Lord Penrhyn's heir on his marriage to William E. Gladstone's niece, Gertrude Glynne, 'a Welsh lady whose family have thrown lustre on Welsh history'. It reminded George Douglas-Pennant (who was unlikely to have forgotten) that he was 'our future master' and expressed the hope that the 'good feeling which exists between employer and employed' would continue. How ironic that this was the man who, as the second Lord Penrhyn, presided over the infamous three-year strike at Penrhyn Quarry, 1900-1903.

Further along the same corridor I found two 1871 water-colours recording the appearance of two of the family's oldest Jamaican plantations, called Denbigh and Pennants, worked with slaves.

Gratitude to the family knew no bounds. Another illuminated address on display records the thanks of the mayor and corporation of Caernarfon to the first Lord Penrhyn for presiding over a fair, held in the town's eisteddfod pavilion in 1883, to raise money for the establishment of a free library which opened the following year, complete with public facilities for all the Caernarfon citizens who did not have bathrooms in their homes.

(APRIL 1992)

PENTREFOELAS

A living heritage village

IF you blink while driving through Pentrefoelas you might never recognise the existence of anything more than a wayside inn, the Foelas Arms. Straddling a cross-roads, astride a straight section of the original A5 post road of 1815, there is here an interesting hamlet built of local stone akin to slate.

Despite evidence of medieval agricultural activity, the present hamlet was developed to cater for the needs of the

London-Holyhead stagecoach traffic, which stopped here from 1745 until the opening of the Chester and Holyhead Railway in 1848.

The oldest date stone – 1815 – is found on the water mill, on the northern side of the road. The mill reopened in 1989 and now produces two specific flours, for bread and pastry. Moreover the miller welcomes visitors to marvel at the mechanical intricacies of some of the oldest technology known to man.

Another date stone (1852) is to be found over the sturdy studded door of the village school, whose porch is still adorned with its original bell, which has not been heard for about eighty years. Wholesome smells coming from the old school provide the only hint of its having been used for the past two decades as a specialised bakery, using traditional recipes and methods to produce tasty cakes which find their way into independent shops as far away as Llandudno and Prestatyn.

Even the redundant Vicarage has been given a new lease of life, as a thriving old people's home. The adjacent church, serving twenty-one members, has recently undergone costly rationalisation, including removal of the leaking belfry and installation of a false ceiling. It was built in 1859 by the Foelas estate, to replace an earlier family chapel. The architect was Sir Gilbert Scott, but it is not one of his best efforts. The church contains some interesting memorials mostly to the Foelas family, whose name changed over the centuries through Griffith, Wynne and Finch to the present Wynne-Finch. The inscriptions remind us that many of them made their careers in the Army. There is a similar reminder on a 1903 ornamental lamp beside the bridge, on the southern arm of the cross-roads.

Inserted into the wall on the opposite side of the bridge there is a plaque telling us: 'This fountain was erected in the year King Edward VII was crowned, 1902'. But the tap has gone, as has the chained lead cup which older residents can remember from before these lawless days of roving thieves and vandals.

Crossing the bridge I was amazed to discover a new stone-built information centre, offering facilities superior to what may be found at many big resorts. It was part of the regeneration and enhancement of this rural community of three hundred and twelve inhabitants into a living heritage village, a project commenced in 1986 by a combination of local government and State agencies.

'By next summer the old Smithy will be in operation, as will several craft workshops in buildings we are now restoring and adapting,' said project manager Berwyn Evans, when I visited the village in 1990. Three years later the project was given the Royal Town Planning Institute's top annual award for good planning. What a pity British Telecom decided to give the village a modern replacement for its perfectly sound red telephone kiosk designed by the church architect's son!

(OCTOBER 1990)

PORTHDINLLAEN

Dreams of Irish wealth

PORTHDINLLAEN (or Portin-llaen), an isolated maritime community of 18 tenanted houses and a pub, was bought by the National Trust in 1994 to prevent its ever being fragmented by individual sales at some future date. In theory it is inaccessible by car except for residents, who no matter how many cars they own, have just one key per household for the locked gates on the road across the spectacular Nefyn golf club, set high on the cliffs above the port. In practice the fairly recent explosion in ownership of four-wheel drive vehicles has resulted in an unwelcome influx of traffic, using low tides to negotiate the mile of beach which forms the normal pedestrian access.

The private road across the golf course dates from 1864, when the lifeboat station was opened on the southern headland which gives Porth Dinllaen its natural shelter from the prevailing winds. In 1804 this shelter, in the otherwise notorious Caernarfon Bay, resulted in Thomas Rogers' plan to create a harbour. Two years later Porthdinllaen Harbour Company was formed, and in 1808 a Bill was presented to Parliament to make this the port for the Irish mail traffic, a move subsequently defeated by only one vote in favour of Caergybi *(Holyhead)*.

With the invention of steam trains Porth Dinllaen again came to the forefront as an alternative to Holyhead, because of the then impossible task of taking a railway across the Menai Strait. The Great Western Railway proposed making Porth Dinllaen the terminus for a line from Worcester via Ludlow, Ffestiniog, Tremadog and Pwllheli. When the rival London and North Western Railway and Robert Stephenson produced their plan for a tubular bridge across the Menai Strait, the Parliamentary vote again went to Holyhead by a majority of one. The tubular bridge was opened in 1850.

Porthdinllaen Harbour Company still exists, now owned by the National Trust. So does its grand office on the sea front, where it was intended to serve as headquarters for the anticipated lucrative Irish traffic which never materialised.

The offices appear to have been built in two phases, now bearing the names of Whitehall and Old Whitehall, forming a single well-built block of interesting houses, with a tunnel running through it to the beach. It used to be a pub, as did Henblas, now a house at the northern extremity of the beach.

'With three pubs this must have been a right merry place,' said one of the residents, after I had trekked across the beach. Only Tŷ Coch survives as a thriving summer pub, with an adequate range of meals. It closes for the winter months. 'How do you get to work?' I enquired of my cheerful waitress. 'Like everyone else, by bike across the sands,' she replied.

Old photographs in the pub remind us of the days when ships were built on the beach – fifty-seven of them over a period of exactly a century, 1776-1876. One of the biggest of the

Porth Dinllaen vessels was the 153-ton brigantine *Fanny Beck*, launched in 1864, and lost with all its crew and passengers on the shores of the Welsh colony in Patagonia in 1879. The last of these vessels, the 149-ton *Annie Lloyd*, sailed the seas until 1907, when it sank with all hands off the Bahamas.

(JULY 1994)

PORTMEIRION

Home for fallen buildings

PORTMEIRION no longer erects memorial plaques for our summers, a kind of meteorological archive which the village's founder, the late Sir Clough Williams-Ellis, started with a plaque dedicated 'To the Summer of 1959, in honour of its splendour'. Twelve years elapsed before he could add '1971, Highly Commended', followed in 1975 by 'Excelled even 1959'. In 1976 he could find no better superlative than 'None such' for the year in which Prime Minister James Callaghan appointed Britain's first Minister for Drought (who became Minister for Floods in the following year). One wonders what Sir Clough might have said for the record summer and winter of 2000!

These delightful plaques are to be found on the stone pillar supporting a bronze statue of Hercules which, like everything else at Portmeirion, had a previous existence elsewhere – in this instance at Aberdeen, where it was first erected in 1850.

The statue is now to be found at the bottom of the garden steps in front of the Town Hall, an ancient-looking building usually known as Hercules Hall, which dates all the way back to 1936-37, which is old in Portmeirion terms. It takes its more familiar name from the fine 1640 vaulted plaster ceiling depicting the labours of Hercules, for which Sir Clough paid £13 to rescue it from the demolition contractors at Emral Hall, at Worthenbury, in Flintshire.

Having cut up the ceiling, for storage at his architectural confection on the shores of the Dwyryd Estuary, Sir Clough then bought wood and stone from Emral with which to create his Town Hall, which he surmounted with an impressive crown – made from a pig-swill boiler. A bust of Sir Clough stands inside the entrance to the Town Hall, flanked by doors to the public lavatories.

Once described by its creator as a 'home for fallen buildings', Portmeirion was built between 1925-39 and 1954-72, to demonstrate that one could develop a very beautiful natural site without defiling it. He built what is now a 'listed' complex which even he, in his latter years, could not alter without Welsh Office permission. Paradoxically it is unlikely that either the local authority or the Welsh Office would ever have given planning permission to create Portmeirion – no such permission being required when Sir Clough began his creation.

Of the resultant product, Socialist philosopher Lord Bertrand Russell once said that as with the Place de l'Opera, in Paris, one only had to sit at Portmeirion to see the whole world go by – now at the rate of 300,000 people a year. When the late Sir Clough introduced charges for seeing what is really an annex to his hotel, his aim was to limit numbers, and the price varied from day to day, or hour to hour. Now everything is on a recognisable commercial footing, with fixed admission charges which are normally reduced by half for the winter months.

As well as the village and its sandy beach, there is a cliff walk and several acres of interesting woodland, within which there is said to be a lake, though it seems impossible to find due to a lack of signposting. Food at the hotel is famous for its excellence but there are less-expensive eating alternatives within the village.

(SEPTEMBER 1992)

POWYS CASTLE.

Clive of India

A CENTURY ago the tenants of Powys Castle estate, close to the Shropshire border, were Welsh-speaking to the point where it was normal to address the Earl of Powis (traditionally misspelt) in their native language.

Among the many illuminated addresses given to the family on special occasions, and now on display for tourists, is one written in Welsh in 1893 by the tenants of Llymystyn and Mathrafal. It congratulates the Earl and Countess on the birth of their heir, Percy, Viscount Clive, and records their gift to the infant of a commemorative gold clock, with the wish that he would live a long and happy life.

He was killed in 1916 on the battlefields of Flanders, while serving with the Scots Guards. Had he lived he would have become the 5th Earl, an inheritance which passed to his brother Mervyn, Viscount Clive, who was killed in action in 1943, without succeeding to the title. For me the challenge of visiting a stately home is to seek out such hidden human stories, which never seem to be given a place in the guidebooks.

The mention of Viscount Clive takes one back to Lord Clive of India, whose son was the first Earl of Powis, hence why a wing of the castle is now devoted to the Clive collection.

Standing on a vantage point just south of Welshpool, and built of red sandstone, most of Powys Castle dates from 1200-1300, but was lived in until just a few years ago. Now in the care of the National Trust, it is frequently open to visitors, complete with ample car park and tea room – with separate and cheaper access for those who just want to see the gardens.

One's exploration begins in the courtyard with its magnificent 3-ton lead statue of Fame born aloft by Pegasus. Nearly 300 years old, it has had many adventures, and different locations within the estate, the fourth Earl's wife being on record as wishing it dead.

Two cannon in the courtyard are part of Clive of India's loot from his defeat of the Sultan of Mysore. They were used to fire a salute to the future Queen Victoria when she visited the castle in 1832, but remained silent when Queen Elizabeth visited Powys Castle in 1989, to review the Royal Welch Fusiliers on the 300th anniversary of the regiment's founding by one of the Powys Castle family.

The official guidebook is worth the price, for a proper tour of the interior, which starts by mounting a flight of 17th century steps from the courtyard. Any visitor must be pleasantly surprised by the comfortable domestic scale of the rooms, tastefully adapted over the centuries to match the 'modern' requirements of each successive era.

In the dining room one can see a happy blend of the fourth Earl's 'modernisation' and some 16th century plaster work in one alcove. The plaster ceiling dates from 1902, copied, according to the Earl's diaries, from the Reindeer Inn, at Banbury. Other ceilings are superbly painted, one made famous by its description in Thomas Pennant's 1776 *Tour in Wales*.

(APRIL 1993)

PRESTATYN

Astride Offa's Dyke

PRESTATYN is a classic example of a seaside resort which grew around its railway station. Although there is evidence of Stone Age, Roman and Norman colonisation, it was the Chester & Holyhead Railway Company who put Prestatyn on the map, in 1848. Twelve years later it became a parish, its church following in 1863.

The original station is intact, externally and internally, an historical gem ignored by resident and visitor alike. It stands to the east of the present station, which was built by the London & North Western Railway Company in 1897. Between the two stations the track is intersected by High Street, which was a level crossing until 1897 – and technically still is for wheelchair users, who can ring a bell to summon assistance from the station, when the gates will be unlocked for what sounds like a somewhat hazardous exercise.

The juxtaposition of the two stations is best seen from the footbridge over the railway. From the bridge one can see clear evidence of the former four tracks, now reduced to two. One of the surplus platforms has been converted into a neat garden, still retaining some of its Victorian furniture.

Coming together in 1897, Queen Victoria's diamond jubilee and the new station gave the impetus for the development of High Street. The old Railway Hotel, south of·the track, was supplemented that year by the much more grand Victoria Hotel, to the north. Like everything else in this spurt of development, the Victoria Hotel was built of red Ruabon glazed brick. Still in good condition, it was converted into flats about six years ago.

The Railway Hotel has retained its original purpose. Apart from having its once-splendid arched doorway bricked up, and new wings added at the sides, it looks much the same as when it was built. However it has changed its name to Offa's Tavern.

Adoption of the name of the famous 8th century king of Mercia is a reminder that Offa's Dyke, marking the Welsh frontier, started from Prestatyn seashore, where there is a new Offa's long distance path information centre, for those who feel like embarking on the 170-mile (273km) walk.

Beside the information centre a barely legible plaque records the visit of the Duke of Gloucester in 1960, for the opening of the Nova pool and recreation centre, since rebuilt and extended in grand Victorian style after the flood damage in 1990.

Returning to High Street, Christ Church, at the top end, is one of the less inspired designs of the prolific T.H. Wyatt. Next to it is the handsome Vicarage built in 1866, and which cost almost as much as the church (£1,250 compared with £1,374).

In front of the high wall surrounding the Vicarage there is a marble fountain in memory of Henry Davis Pochin 'who by his foresight, public spirit and useful work initiated the development of Prestatyn'. The same Mr Pochin is best remembered as the founder of Bodnant, and its magnificent gardens, in Dyffryn Conwy, from where his daughter married the man who became the first Lord Aberconway.

(APRIL 1994)

RED WHARF BAY

Where the Thetis was beached

RED WHARF BAY, or Traeth Coch in Welsh, was once known as Porthllongdy, which would have looked rather silly if bilingualised into Port Shiphouse. Several robust buildings from the harbour's days as a modest shipbuilding, quarrying and smuggling centre are still in use, one bearing the date-stone 1778.

The more familiar name describes the huge expanse of sand exposed at low tide, on a shallow shelf in a bay some three miles (5km) long and a mile (1.6km) wide, which floods very quickly. For those aware of the tidal perils it is a superb playground, whose sea front has a hotel at one end and an inn at the other.

Beach and promenade are at the end of a narrow twisting road out of Pentraeth (meaning End of the Beach). Best seen in the winter, Red Wharf Bay's summer popularity can be gauged from the notice on the Ship Inn's menu board: 'During our regular busy periods a long delay is unavoidable'.

Ancient man appears to have occupied the limestone headland at the northern end, which looks like a medieval fort, hence its name, Castell Mawr. Thanks to careless handling of their coins, we know the Romans used the headland, and probably the harbour.

Beyond the headland lies Traeth Bychan where the submarine HMS *Thetis* was beached, still with ninety-nine bodies on board, after being raised five months after she failed to surface during her trials off Llandudno in 1939. She was returned to the Birkenhead yard of Cammell Laird, from where she re-emerged in 1940 as HMS *Thunderbolt*, only to be sunk by an Italian corvette in 1943.

More famous in the local folk memory is the 1859 wrecking of the *Royal Charter*, at Moelfre, with the loss of four hundred and forty-four lives. Her name is recorded on the front of the Ship Inn, a reminder that bodies were washed ashore in the bay.

Most of the bay is in the parish of Pentraeth where, in St Mary's churchyard, one can still see the small slate tombstones of two unidentified *Royal Charter* victims recorded simply as No. 5 and No. 6. They are on the opposite side of the path from the big Celtic cross memorials of the Panton/Vivian family, of Plas Gwyn, a Georgian house a short distance from the church, on the Beaumaris road.

The parish name was originally Llanfair Betws Geraint. Much fun is made of Welsh as being a long winded language, but to convey those three two-syllable words in English needs all of 'the Holy Enclosure of Geraint's Bede House dedicated to St Mary'. There has been considerable speculation as to the identity of Geraint and his saintly reputation.

Three famous stones can be seen in the field known as Cae Tair Naid *(field of three leaps)* beside the entrance to Plas Gwyn drive. Remarkably small in relation to their ancient fame, the stones are said to mark the scene of a contest of three leaps, staged in medieval times to decide who should marry the grand-daughter of Geraint. Hywel, son of Owain Gwynedd, won and the stones commemorate his prowess – as well as the failure of his rival, who died of a broken heart.

(MARCH 1992)

RHOS-ON-SEA (LLANDRILLO-YN-RHOS)

Rhos Fynach

RHOS FYNACH, a 15th century building which had been boarded up for five years, was extended and converted into a pub and restaurant during 1990-92, to serve the popular promenade and new-found harbour at Rhos-on-Sea. Thus it was saved from the demolition which Colwyn Borough Council, and its Colwyn Bay predecessor, had been threatening since 1971.

It retains sufficient of its original structure to cause one to ponder about the origins of its strange name, which can be translated as Monk's Marsh or Monk's Moor, both of which might be completely wrong. The earliest known documentary reference to the place was in 1230, when Llywelyn ap Iorwerth (the Great) recorded that all rights in the land of *'Ros Veneych'* had been bought by his chief executive, Ednyfed Fychan (ancestor of the Tudors, whose medieval palace may still be found in the trees on the nearby slopes of Bryn Euryn).

In suggesting that Llywelyn bought a place already called Rhos Fynach to give it to the monks of Aberconwy Abbey (which he founded on the site of the present Conwy parish church), the Royal Commission on Ancient Monuments has, of course, ruined the oft-repeated argument that its name perpetuates its ownership by the monks.

The Welsh word 'rhos' would describe the nearby former wetlands astride Afon Ganol, now mostly culverted across Rhos-on-Sea golf course. That topographical description may also have given the administrative name to the Cantref of Rhos used for the wider area surrounding Afon Ganol.

But what if the similarity of name is coincidental? Take a walk to the beach, near Rhos Fynach, for a few minutes contemplation in the ancient six-seater Chapel of St Trillo where holy communion is occasionally celebrated. Though just above high water mark, the well beneath the chapel altar

193

always contains fresh water, regarded as miraculous by some but a commonplace topographical juxtaposition for those of us who acquired primitive survival skills while soldiering in Palestine.

Looking for other Mediterranean clues perhaps one should remember the Arabic word 'ras,' the Hebrew 'rosh,' or even the Irish 'ross' – all of which mean 'headland'. Then we can visualise the 6th century Celtic evangelist Trillo's arrival on this shore, where he provided himself with a well, a home and a fish trap, to spend many years farming his 'llan,' or enclosure – hence the proper Welsh name for this parish: Llandrillo-yn-rhos.

Presumably unable to distinguish between a holy hermit and a monk, the people would describe the area as Rhos Fynach, which means 'the monk's headland' – at least that is my theory, and first plausible explanation for the name of the present 15th century house, with later extensions built in association with a prolific fish trap which existed on the shore until World War One.

Dudley, Earl of Leicester, favourite of Queen Elizabeth I, once owned Rhos Fynach, but conveyed it to Morgan ap John, a master mariner, in 1575 – the original deeds were displayed at the house until the end of the 19th century. Probably thatched in its original state, the old stone building was given a roof of Bethesda slates at the beginning of the 20th century, a feature which would have been restored during the most recent restaurant conversion, but for the interfering Ancient Monuments Society, who wanted incongruous English stone 'slates'.

(SEPTEMBER 1990)

RHOSNEIGR

It just grew

RHOSNEIGR was never planned: it just grew, in whichever direction anyone cared to lay a new cul-de-sac in the sand dunes, or squeeze a new road between existing houses.

In 1941 the straggling community gave its name to a new fighter airfield, built to defend Liverpool against Luftwaffe attacks from Brittany, but after joking about the pronunciation of RAF Rhosneigr for two months, the Air Ministry decided to call it RAF Valley. The airfield site was nearly lost in 1897 to the Welsh Explosives Company, who wanted to build a factory for the manufacture of gelignite. Opponents successfully argued that Rhosneigr was a new fast-growing holiday resort.

Such a possibility had been foreseen as long ago as 1863, when the present Maelog Lake Hotel was built on the common. The encroachment is shrouded in mystery, for unlike the majority of 'tai unos' (that is, a house built in the course of a single night) with which ancient Welsh law enabled common land to be colonised, Maelog was not sufficiently remote to escape notice – temperance zealots from neighbouring Llanfaelog burnt it down midway through its first construction. Maelog Lake Hotel now appears to be the oldest surviving building in Rhosneigr, though photographs exist of at least one neighbouring smallholding known to have been in existence as early as 1830.

Rhosneigr was still a scattered hamlet when the lifeboat house was built in 1872, after a series of spectacular shipwrecks on the treacherous rocks which give the beach so much of its character for modern tourists. Few residents can now direct a stranger to the lifeboat house which closed in 1924. I asked nineteen people before finding the answer in the pharmacy. Once found, it is unmistakable, its access to the sea partially blocked by a grassed mound of new dune.

Withdrawal of the lifeboat did not end the humanitarian

gallantry of the men of Rhosneigr. A plaque erected in 1989 at the Coast Guard hut recalls a drama in 1941, after a Botha aircraft, manned by a Polish crew from the nearby airfield, came down in the sea in a ferocious gale. During the next few minutes eleven men were drowned in a series of vain attempts to rescue the three airmen. The RNLI awarded each a posthumous bronze medal. Two 17-years-old survivors each received the George Medal and RNLI silver medal.

Rhosneigr's serious bid to become a tourist centre began in 1907, with the opening of the railway station. The station still exists, or more accurately two stations, one on either side of the track, each served by a separate road. A notice on each unmanned platform tells intending travellers to make clear signals to approaching drivers, some of whom will stop on request (depending upon their time table). Make sure you find the correct approach road, for another notice warns that crossing the track can incur a fine of £200.

A sign of the times is the once famous Bay Hotel, opened at the beginning of the last century, licensed two decades later, but now fenced off and derelict.

(FEBRUARY 1994)

RHUDDLAN CASTLE

Birthplace of the Prince of Wales

RHUDDLAN Castle reopened to the public in 1993 after being closed for four years for emergency repairs. Within weeks a notice was placed on one tower saying: 'We apologise that this area is temporarily closed due to vandalism.'

Visitors may wonder how the castle is still standing. After the Civil War, in which it was held for King Charles, Parliament decreed it should be made untenable, thus starting the process of removing stones from the lower courses of the towers, which were used as a quarry for another couple of centuries.

Parliament paid insufficient regard to the tenacity of medieval mortar, for none of the towers collapsed, even if they do look as though they have been gnawed by some enormous rat.

The castle is still surrounded by its original outer curtain wall and neatly-revetted moat, which was always dry. At the southern corner the curtain wall has additional fortification, including a four-storey tower, to protect the dock gate into the castle's tidal berth off Afon Clwyd, which was here straightened into a new course and widened, to link the garrison to the sea at Rhyl.

What I found fascinating, standing on the medieval quayside, was the realisation that the warships of Edward I's formidable fleet must have been very small, to tie up here. They could have been no bigger than a Conwy trawler of today.

Rhuddlan castle predates Edward's final conquest of 1282, and once marked England's frontier with Wales, sulking on the opposite side of the river. Construction began in 1277. King Edward and Queen Eleanor turned up a year later to survey the work, and perhaps give final instructions for the royal apartments. The towers were roofed with lead in 1280, and the King's Hall with timber in 1281.

Surviving documentation for its construction shows that work stopped in 1282 – obviously because of the Welsh attack which began Llywelyn ap Gruffudd's final and fatal war, which resulted in the annexation of his country. The war damage bill has survived, as have the accounts for lavish provision of the Queen's apartments, including a private chapel, and the 1283 construction of a workshop for the Queen's goldsmith. All that evidence lends credence to the belief that Caernarfon's claim to have been the birthplace of the first English Prince of Wales – the basis for Prince Charles's ceremonial investiture in 1969 – is quite spurious.

Caernarfon castle would have been little more than a pile of stones when the first prince was born, to fulfil the King's promise to present the Welsh with a native-born prince who spoke no English. The Queen's confinement could have been accommodated comfortably and safely at Rhuddlan, where some of her household was in residence.

The garrison gave its name to the famous Statute of Rhuddlan of 1284, which made Ynys Môn, Gwynedd and Ceredigion subject to English criminal law, though leaving Welsh common law and the Welsh language intact. It was only when the Welsh Tudors seized the English crown, three centuries later, that the Welsh language was outlawed – the relevant clause of the Act of Union of 1536 remaining unrepealed until as recently as 1967.

(JULY 1993)

RHYL

The Sea Life Centre

'WELCOME to a wondrous underwater world where thousands of astonishing sea creatures from around our shores await your discovery. Prepare to be amazed by creatures you never guessed existed.'

So says the greeting as one begins to journey through Rhyl Sea Life Centre. Before the advent of the car and, to a lesser extent, the train, Wales was essentially a maritime nation, with most of its population distributed around the coast, and a harbour in every usable bay, creek or estuary.

Even half a century ago Welsh children were very knowledgeable about the natural wildlife to be found along our beaches, with Sunday school trips to the seaside spreading the message to those who lived inland. Those simple pleasures of yesteryear were recreated in 1993 for a new generation of car-borne children, in the £1.4m investment which features, among other things, Wales's first walk-through aquarium tunnel.

Viewed from the outside, the new building on Rhyl promenade has no hope of ever winning either an environmental or an architectural award, but such considerations never seem to have mattered in this brash resort. Inside it is indeed a new wonderland, based entirely on some seventy species of wildlife to be found around our own shores, assembled in ten displays commencing with a salutary reminder of 'The impact of man'.

As well as a wooden groyne stretching up a beach, to remind us of man's constant battle to preserve his domain from the sea, there is the man-made debris, such as plastic bottles and beer cans, with which the top of the animal chain pollutes the environment of the very place from which life originated.

We are reminded, too, that man is not the only land species put at risk by his own muck, for the shoreline is scavenged during the night by creatures such as foxes and hedgehogs.

Animated by skilful reproduction of natural sea movement, the various displays range from the rock pools we can all explore, through the less accessible deep sea nooks and crannies, to a display where day is turned into night to explore the species which are nocturnally active.

There are natural biological curiosities, such as the cuckoo wrasse. They all start life as females with a life expectancy of about seventeen years. In mid-life a proportion turn male, change colour and build a nest into which females are enticed to perpetuate the species.

Man has always interfered with nature and so there is a display devoted to myth and mystery, including photographs of the mummified Japanese mermaids which turned up as museum exhibits in the 19th century. They look realistic enough, but are now known to be a skilful combination of monkey, lizard, cat and fish. Tales of sea monsters like the kraken, a giant octopus claimed to have been seen by several sailors of a century ago, are explored – and who is to say what might lurk undiscovered in the deepest depths of the oceans?

(MARCH 1993)

RHYL

Foryd harbour

FORYD harbour, straddling Afon Clwyd, was the womb from which the brash and ungrateful resort of Rhyl was born. It is still possible to step back in time at the Foryd, and if one approaches from the west, and stops short of crossing the 1932 bridge, it is never necessary to set foot in Rhyl.

The ugly steel bridge, painted a garish bright blue, is almost unique in not being endorsed with the names of the council chairman and his stalwarts; not even the name of the contractor, nor the supplier of the steel. Perhaps none wanted to be associated with it.

Upstream one can see the stone piers of the earlier toll bridge of 1860, which could be swung open for shipping, as could a section of the 1848 railway bridge a little higher up. Vessels were then able to navigate Afon Clwyd as far as Rhuddlan, whose medieval castle still incorporates a dock designed to house the navy of Edward I, built long before he had conquered Wales.

The rutted and collapsing west bank road, south of the present bridge, is the remains of the pre-1932 highway to Rhyl. Behind the modern dwelling bearing the name of Old Toll House one can catch a glimpse of the old Lifeboat House, from the days when everything centred on the harbour.

Now a builder's workshop, it still bears a plaque recording it was the 'Rhyl Lifeboat Establishment', given in 1868 by Miss Helen Hodgson, of Edgbaston, executrix of Mrs Elizabeth Morgan, of Cheltenham. There are no hints, though, that it was erected to house one of the most historic boats in the history of the RNLI, the 'tubular lifeboat' exhibited at London's Great Exhibition of 1851 by Henry Richardson, of Bala, and his son Thomas Richardson, of Pwllheli. Designed on the catamaran principle, it was their challenge to the disaster-prone 'self-righting' boats of the period. It was placed at the Foryd in 1856, named the *Elizabeth Morgan* in 1867, and remained in service until 1893.

Virtually all maritime activity is now concentrated north of the bridge, where archaeologists have suddenly become very excited about a wreck of which only the spars can be seen at low tide. Lying off the eastern shore, a stone's throw from the funfair, it is believed to be the *City of Ottawa*, the last 'surviving' Canadian-built full-rigged wooden ship, built at Quebec in 1860, and removed from Lloyd's register in 1897.

The Foryd was the base of the pioneering steam submarine *Resurgam*, invented by a Liverpool curate, the Revd George Garrett, and built at Birkenhead in 1879. The three-man crew used the Foryd for several weeks of sea trials, but abandoned their 41-ft (12.5m) vessel between Rhyl and Llandudno, during a storm in February 1880, leaving it to vanish until December 1995 when the unmistakable submarine snagged a fishing net.

The Foryd's best-kept secret is its promenade, reached via a public footpath and an appallingly unnecessary patch of mud behind the Ferry Hotel.

(JANUARY 1993)

RUABON

Gateway to fantasy

'ACCESS allowed by permit only,' says the notice confronting anyone who dares walk through the derelict arched gateway at the end of Ruabon's Park Street. The curious are directed to buy their permits (which used to cost 50p) from the Wynnstay Estate Office, in Church Street, a reminder that this was once the gateway to the home of the Williams-Wynn family, whose baronetcy dates from 1688.

They sold the house (rebuilt after an 1858 fire) and 150 acres of garden for £18,000 in 1950, to Lindisfarne boys' school, who held an annual open day every May for anyone who wanted to see some of the past glories of Wynnstay Park. For the other 364 days one had to make do with the limited view from Ruabon – or more accurately Rhiwabon – whose stone gateway was built in 1783. The present iron gates are a 1912 replacement, given by Wrexham Borough to mark the coming of age of the future 8th baronet. The wheel and mechanism for operating the original gates could be seen until about 1980 inside the neighbouring Gate House, now privately owned.

Today the ever-open gateway leads to nothing more than an abandoned piece of overgrown driveway, separated from Wynnstay by the deep cutting of the Rhiwabon bypass road, opened some eighteen years ago. No bailiffs will appear if you ignore the notice at the entrance to what has all the potential of a public park – if the community cared to do something about it. Wandering to the edge of the cutting you can see the avenue of trees on the other side, marking the old drive.

In the trees, near the modern roundabout in the foreground, lies the pre-1784 bath-house, which visitors to Wynnstay once had to use before proceeding to the mansion. To the right stands the 100-ft (30m) high column, surmounted by a bronze urn, designed by James Wyatt to commemorate the death in 1789 of the 4th baronet. The internal staircase was closed several years ago. The column still stands on Williams-Wynn farmland, as do the remains of Nant-y-belan tower erected in memory of the five officers and thirty-nine men of the Ancient British Cavalry, killed in Northern Ireland in 1798. The regiment of over three hundred was raised in North Wales by Sir Watkin Williams-Wynn (all the sons are called Watkin) to defend Britain against the French, but found itself fighting Catholics at the Battle of Arklow.

A more lasting memorial is the blood-stained hand of Ulster, escutcheoned on the signboard of the Wynnstay Arms, next door to the old cavalry armoury in Park Street. How remarkable, therefore, that St. Mary's church, across the road, should display a notice saying the 19th century building (with 14th century tower) is now shared by Protestants and Catholics, using a time table as carefully structured as that of the rival custodians of the Church of the Holy Sepulchre, in Jerusalem. Unfortunately on the day I called the church was locked to everyone.

(MARCH 1991)

17 RUE MONTOYER

Little Wales in Brussels

HIDDEN in the Brussels diplomatic quarter, 17 rue Montoyer was an unexpected corner of Wales in which we all had a share until the year 2000, by way of council taxes, VAT or other State taxes. This is the nearest Wales has yet come to an embassy abroad, an image enhanced by the visitor's discovery, outside the front door, of two parking spaces marked 'CD', permanently reserved for cars with Diplomatic Corps number plates in this city of muddled politics.

Rue Montoyer is a broad street of granite setts. One block away from No 17, only the Palais des Academies separates it from the Parc du Bruxelles, where the defeat of the Dutch army in 1830 created the Kingdom of the Belgians.

A plaque erected by the Society of Belgian Architects informs us the street was named after Louis Joseph Montoyer, 1747-1811, designer of some of the city's most famous buildings during its Austrian and early French periods of foreign government. One wonders what Montoyer would have to say about today's purely functional architecture of the countless concrete offices in the street named in his honour.

In the midst of concrete uniformity the Wales European Centre stood out at 17 rue Montoyer, not as a thing of beauty, but for its dark glass facade, unbroken by steel or stone for all its nine floors. Tenants were listed inside the marble foyer, revealing the real reason for the Diplomatic Corps parking spaces: the embassy of Papua New Guinea had the ground floor; and the embassy and consulate of Chile were on the third floor. Freistaates Bayern (Bavarian Free State) had the fourth and fifth floors but did not enjoy diplomatic status, which is reserved for Federal Germany, whose embassy is elsewhere.

Canolfan Ewropeaidd Cymru was listed for the sixth floor where, on leaving the lift, one saw a plaque of distinctive blue-grey Blaenau Ffestiniog slate, recording its unveiling during the official opening by Welsh Secretary David Hunt in 1992, when I attended as one of the EC Press Corps (whose watering hole, in the Brussels Press Club, rejoices in the name of Jones's Bar). Pointing to the Red Dragon, draped on a lobby wall, director John Gibney apologised: 'If there was any way of erecting a flagpole we would fly it outside.' Even the Dragon in the hall vanished a few weeks later, after the Bavarians protested to the landlord.

Representing a bilingual country within a bilingual city, the full long-winded title of this tiny corner of Wales was: Wales European Centre; Canolfan Ewropeaidd Cymru; La Mission Européenne du Pays de Galles; De Europese Missie van Wales. A seasonal vase of daffodils used to stand on the front reception desk, where the informative literature included 'The Welsh Ambassador', an appropriately named overseas news-sheet, published by the Welsh Development Agency, who funded the Centre jointly with local authorities, training and enterprise councils and sections of the University of Wales.

The Centre comprised four offices, a conference room and auxiliary rooms where everything, including Cariad wine, grown and bottled in Glamorgan, reminded the visitor he was in a tiny corner of Cymru, at the centre of the European Union.

In September 1994 the Welsh Guards were feted in Brussels on the 50th anniversary of the regiment's liberation of the city from German occupation. The British Ambassador to Belgium during the celebrations was Llanelli-born John W.D. Gray, from

Brecon, who entertained me at the Embassy.

With the birth of the Welsh Assembly the Wales European Centre moved to new premises in 2000 but the pioneering office at 17 rue Montoyer has earned a permanent place in Welsh history as Wales's first overseas diplomatic mission station, albeit a status recognised only in its French and Flemish titles.

(FEBRUARY 1993)

SELATTYN

Little Wales in England

SELATTYN is technically in Shropshire, but everything about it, including its name, reminds us it used to be in Wales – and was part of the diocese of St. Asaph until as recently as 1920, when it was transferred to Lichfield.

In a Wales accustomed to an English version surviving at the expense of a Welsh place name, it comes as something of a surprise to realise the very opposite has happened at Selattyn! It is surrounded by communities bearing such names as Rhos, Wern, Hengoed, Pantglas, Nant, and many more, all of them in what is now England in this once volatile border territory.

Most of the village's houses bear Welsh names, such as Tanyfedw and Ynyshir. At the first house on which I called I found an English owner delighted with an opportunity to practice his Welsh, which he had learnt to an extraordinary degree of perfection by attending night classes in Oswestry, which is also in Shropshire.

This is a small community of neat genteel houses, among which I was surprised to find a young woman pouring a big can of white paint on to the middle of the road.

'Why are you doing that?' I asked. 'To cover the fish,' she replied, as she and I leapt to safety while a van splashed its way through the mess. She disappeared into a nearby house while unexpectedly heavy traffic spread the paint the length and breadth of the road – and most of the way to Offa's Dyke. All became clear when I enquired at a house, to be told the woman had obliterated an ichthys, the fish symbol which the ancient Greeks had used as a secret code for Christ – the Greek word for fish spells out the initial letters of their version of 'Jesus Christ, Son of God, Saviour'.

Seemingly the ichthys had been painted on Selattyn's only road by the organisers of that week's Christian gypsy festival, on farm land at nearby Bronygarth, where many hundreds of vehicles, including caravans, lorries, and general utility vans were assembled – with the declared intention of dispersing at the weekend.

'Selattyn is not the place for this kind of nonsense; our road is much too narrow for this sort of traffic – over five hundred vehicles turned up on the very first day,' said one angry resident. In fact Selattyn does have an old gypsy link which may not be known to the festival organisers. The parish register contains an entry made in 1715 for the baptism of Bohemia, son of Abraham Wood, 'King of ye Gypsyes'.

The village has a rather fine old church, first mentioned in the *Taxatio* of 1291, and much altered over the years, with the addition of a tower in 1703. Its chancel has a superb 15th century vaulted roof, revealed when later lath and plaster was removed during major restoration in 1891, for which there is a brass plate commemorating its reopening by Lord Harlech. Selattyn has one pub, though it was closed when I called in search of a lunchtime snack.

(JULY 1994)

SODOM

Cream teas in the surgery

DO NOT look back when you get to Sodom, lest you should be frozen into a pillar of steel, to match the ugly television transmitting masts dominating Moel-y-parc, on the other side of the Wheeler Valley. Welsh Victorians had a panache for allocating Biblical place names, and were usually making a subtle comment on a community or its topography. As there is nothing in the Welsh Sodom that remotely resembles the hot barren desert of the Palestinian original, one is prompted to ask why this scattered community was once considered extraordinarily wicked?

Whatever the cause, its sins have long been forgotten, and Sodom's very existence is now in danger of going the same way, a sinner from elsewhere having stolen the old roadside boundary name plate.

That Sodom predates the Victorians is evident from its two modernised long-houses, probably built in the 17th century. The Welsh long-house was a cosy dairy farming arrangement whereby a family and its cattle shared the same roof, at opposite ends of a rectangular building. An open door from the house to the byre gave the family two useful benefits: the abundant body heat of the cows and the accompanying stench, which masked their own body odours.

Even older are the Iron Age earthworks on Moel-y-Gaer, the adjoining hill one passes when negotiating the exceedingly narrow twisting roads north of Bodfari, in search of Sodom. Though Sodom and Sodom's Covert are indelibly preserved on the Ordnance Survey, the score, or thereabouts, houses are so scattered that it is difficult to identify this hillside community. Only on my second attempt did I chance to stop outside Fronhaul, where Mrs Gwladys Edwards assured me I was in the middle of Sodom.

'The only explanation I have ever heard for the name is that the people of these parts were once very quarrelsome,' she said, adding that it did not seem a very good explanation.

Though road signs no longer point to it, the name on the map is sufficient to attract a steady trickle of curious visitors throughout the year. 'I do a steady turn over in Welsh teas, which I serve in the old operating theatre,' said Mrs Edwards. Its white wall tiles and adjoining scrub-up room, still with its old plumbing and 'sterile' cupboards, testify to Fronhaul's former use, when it was the home, surgery and hospital of eye surgeon Farington Marsden Granger, a Boer War veteran who died in 1932.

Mrs Edwards remembers the days when this remote community had its own Baptist place of worship, officially named Salem but always called Sodom Chapel. Now converted into a house, the 1848 building still has the original Welsh inscription over the door, which translates as: 'Watch your step when you visit the house of God'.

No one could tell me why one of the community's oldest houses, at the start of the hill up to Sodom, is called Olivet – the word usually applied in Jerusalem to the Garden of Gethsemene, at the foot of the Mount of Olives.

(MAY 1991)

SOUTHSEA

The forgotten village

SOUTHSEA is a forgotten village, said the Vicar, the Revd Richard Parry, at a community meeting at Berea chapel, in 1992. Knowing that Berea was the Biblical town where 'they came to stir up trouble and rouse the rabble', I went in search of a place so forgotten that it had even escaped the attentions of the Welsh Language Society.

Southsea lies some 2½ miles (4km) WNW of Wrexham town

centre. In 1903 historian Alfred Palmer said it was 'an absurd name which should never have been adopted, especially as there was an appropriate name ready to hand in Glanyrafon, the appellation of two old farms'. The farms were on either side of the now virtually dry Afon Gwenfro, west of the superfluous Great Western Railway bridge which divides the community, despite the pedestrian subway provided in the 1970s – the subway was intended to eliminate the hazard of walking under the bridge.

'The bridge is a useless reminder of the community's past industrial wealth, and people will not use the subway even in daytime,' said the Vicar, adding: 'The lights are broken, it stinks of urine, and graffiti covers the walls'.

Southsea developed around an inn of that name (originally two words: South Sea) at Glanyrafon, which was first shown in the rate books of 1786, – rather far removed from the 1720 affair of the South Sea Bubble, which Palmer thought the inn commemorated. In 1881 the rate books start using the single word Southsea.

A favourite explanation is that the inn was founded by a sailor who had happy thoughts of Southsea, in Portsmouth. The name of the pub was changed to The Ship, which was demolished in about 1882 to make way for the Wrexham Mold & Connah's Quay Railway. The WM&CQ Railway used to have its own bridge over the road. It was demolished to make way for a new road to Brymbo steelworks, which closed in 1990.

A little way beyond is All Saints Church, whose board tells us it serves the grouped parishes of Berse Drelincourt, Southsea and Tanyfron. 'It is all a little confusing for Berse Drelincourt is actually in Caego(f), which is grouped with New Broughton, where I am also Vicar,' said Mr Parry, adding that for good measure he was Vicar of the independent parish of Pentre Broughton.

Mary Drelincourt was the widow of a Dean of Armagh. The chapel of ease bearing her name was built in 1742 and consecrated in 1759. Southsea's first church was built in 1884, seven years after the opening of Plas Power colliery (which closed in 1938). Subsidence caused its replacement during 1925-28 but this church suffered the same problem and was demolished in 1984, when the congregation moved across the road to the former church hall, now serving a dual role and thriving.

Nonconformists, who once had several chapels in the village, are now served only by Berea United Reformed church, which was reduced to four members and a long-retired minister who gives them a service once a month when I last visited it in 1992. Its 1904 foundation stones are all inscribed in Welsh, one having been laid by Samuel Moss, the local MP, but the services are now in English – and the community would like the chapel to be converted for dual use, similar to All Saints.

(OCTOBER 1992)

ST ASAPH

The hidden city

SAINT ASAPH is a web of historic streets and interesting footpaths, all hidden from those who know the tiny city as nothing more than a cathedral, a hill and a maternity hospital. The natives even have their own well-attended parish church, operating at the bottom of the hill in opposition to the cathedral at the top. The southern door bears the date 1687, but is inaccessible behind the permanently locked gate on a porch added during general restoration in 1872.

Among the repositioned stones in the now neatly lawned cemetery, one stands apart – that of Richard Jones, 1780-1843, better known as Dic Aberdaron. This barefooted, unkempt wandering beggar was fluent in Welsh, English, Latin, Greek,

Hebrew, Arabic and many ancient dead languages of the Middle East, but could find no one to publish his life's work, a Welsh-Greek-Hebrew dictionary.

Nearby Mill Street no longer has its water mill but it does lead to a footpath along the banks of Afon Elwy. Shortly after passing under the 1969 bridges of the A55 by-pass, a stepped path to the right eventually leads to a bridge over the A55, ending in Mount Road – which leads to the cathedral.

Just a short distance along Mount Road a lane to the left leads past the new cemetery gates to a stile and signposted footpath. I took the path, as instructed by two kindly ladies, to the barely negotiable remains of a footbridge beneath the oak tree at the bottom of the field, and thence over another stile.

It was the recommended route to Pont Dafydd, built in 1630, and now marooned in the middle of a soggy field, complete with two walls and cobbled surface. Here, apparently, was where Felicia Dorothea Hemans sat to write her most famous words: *The boy stood on the burning deck whence all but he had fled.* The poem was inspired by the death of the nine-year-old son of the captain of Napoleon's flagship, the *Orient*, at the Battle of the Nile in 1798.

Her home was at the nearby Bronwylfa, which has given its name to Bronwylfa Square, where I found the city's old Independent chapel, taken over by the Presbyterians in 1968 – when they abandoned their own enormous edifice, in the street known as Y Gemig. The old Baptist church, also in Y Gemig, has been converted into flats. Tucked away and out of sight at the top of Y Gemig is St. Asaph's oldest inn, the Red Lion. It displays a programme testifying to its use as a theatre in 1806.

Jesuit Fathers established a Roman Catholic church in Chester Road in 1854. Beyond it is the 1853 Court House, now a youth club, complete with stone carvings of the royal arms. Nearby are brick buttresses marking the site of a bridge which used to carry the Rhyl-Corwen railway. Between the buttresses are what may be the country's last example of plated holes laid in the roads in 1940, ready to house hairpin-shaped pieces of railway line – to impede the progress of German tanks in the event of an invasion.

(MAY 1992)

ST GEORGE

H.R.H. and Alice's cousin

SAINT GEORGE, near Abergele, is not named after the Iraqi-born patron saint of England, who is buried at Lydda and never knew that England even existed, but after Edward I's Alpine-born castle architect, James of St George. That, however, does not explain why its name fails to appear on any sign for traffic coming from the west, and neither is there an obvious exit by which to reach it. Only when travelling towards the west along the A55 expressway will you see the bilingual sign (on which the Welsh was corrected in 1990) to 'St. George/Llan San Siôr, ½ mile' (800m).

It is thought that James of St George took up residence here after the completion of Conwy castle, and that he lies buried within the grounds of the parish church, which displays a list of rectors dating back to 1278. He must turn in his grave every time he contemplates the appalling architecture of the present church bearing his name (but dedicated to St George of Lydda). One does not even recognise it as a church when driving up the lane into the village. It was completed in 1894, to replace a Norman two-nave building of which there is an illustration in stained glass, in a four-light window commemorating the 1920 transfer from Lytham St Annes to Bodelwyddan Castle of Lowther College (which closed in 1982).

Oddly enough there is nothing in the church to commemorate rival Clarendon School's twenty-seven years at Kinmel Hall – whose Victorian occupants laid a special secondary drive straight to the church. Clarendon School left

Kinmel in 1975 after a disastrous fire, caused by a forgotten electric boiling ring in one of the dormitories. When first spotted by a cleaner the fire was confined to some furniture but by the end of the day much of the fine old building had become a roofless ruin.

The gateposts of the church drive to Kinmel still display the shared coat of arms of Hugh Robert Hughes – who enjoyed being known as HRH – and his wife Florentia Liddell, whose great-grandfather (Sir Henry George Liddell) was also the great-grandfather of Alice Liddell, of Wonderland fame. The same device can be found inside the church, in the graveyard and on the outer wall of the village hall, where an inscribed stone tells us it was built in 1899 by Lady Florentia Hughes. It is not, however, displayed next door, at the neat Kinmel Arms, a very popular eating place which looks far too sedate for a pub.

Kinmel Hall, hidden in its own park land, has been rebuilt since the 1975 fire, to look much the same as when W.E. Nesfield rebuilt it during 1871-74. The house has had a mixed existence. After ceasing to be a family home in 1929 it became a boys' school, then a treatment spa (run by Florence Lindley, founder headmistress of Lowther College), a military hospital, a hotel and osteopathic centre, and then a girls' school in 1948. It served as a Christian conference centre until 2000, and is now empty.

(DECEMBER 1990)

TALACRE

A rich cocktail of fuels

TALACRE, now a new oil and gas terminal for Liverpool Bay, has always been a strange mixture of intensive industry and rustic simplicity. Durable but easily dressed Talacre sandstone provided material for the walls of such places as Basingwerk Abbey, St Asaph Cathedral and St Winifred's well.

Coal was discovered at nearby Mostyn at least as early as 1640, when a 15 ft (4.6m) seam was being mined at a depth of some 150 ft (45m), despite methane problems. Midway through the 19th century the Mostyn coal measures were finished, prompting the new Lord Mostyn to look for replacement mineral royalties a little to the north, at what is variously described as Point of Ayr/Air/Ayre or Talacre.

Coal was located at 300 ft ((90m) beneath the surface in 1865 and, after a false start by the Prestatyn Colliery Company, and several years of litigation, the West Mostyn Colliery Company was formed in 1873 to exploit the find until they struck geological problems two years later. The more familiar name of Point of Ayr Colliery came into use in 1884, to give us the last survivor of the North Wales coal mines until it, too, closed in the mid 1990's. The site has been cleared and there are now proposals to mark it with a memorial.

Adjacent to the colliery site there was a novel liquefaction plant, designed during a pessimistic period of complex Arabian politics, to create expensive Welsh oil from coal waste. That, too, closed soon after the colliery.

Talacre's hidden cocktail of natural fuel extends out to sea as coal, and beyond into Liverpool Bay as gas, with oil under the Dee Estuary and out to the north. Lead ore was also found in these parts., and all this activity has given Talacre the appearance of a Welsh Klondyke.

It has a tatty mixture of wooden and asbestos shacks, a few tiny bungalows, unsurfaced muddy roads with grand names, and lots of caravans, all thrown together without anything resembling an overall plan. In summer this hotchpotch springs to life with hundreds of holidaymakers, hence the incongruous abundance of licensed premises in this otherwise sparsely populated churchless community.

Talacre was not always churchless. Benedictine nuns took over its 1829 hillside mansion of the same name in 1920, and built a church in 1932, adding the campanile in 1952. They left in 1988 and Talacre Abbey is now a private house. It was originally the home of the Roman Catholic branch of the Mostyn family, which produced some famous soldiers.

Winter is the best time to visit Talacre, enabling one to explore in peace its sand dunes, beach and treacherous sea-marsh with RSPB bird watching hide. Strangers must be surprised to find an old lighthouse on the beach. A three-storey coal-fired lighthouse was built here in 1777, by Joseph Turner, of Whitchurch, and some would claim it was incorporated in the present building, dating from about 1824 and attributed to Robert Stevenson, grandfather of author Robert Louis Stevenson.

In 1844 a cast-iron replacement lighthouse was built nearer the mouth of the Dee but has now vanished. Also lost in the sand is the lifeboat house, from where the first recorded rescue was made in 1835. The station closed in 1923 but its 1895-1916 boat survived until 1940 as a fund-raising exhibit on Colwyn Bay promenade. It was finally removed and destroyed lest it should be of use either to invading German troops or to escaping spies seeking to rendezvous with U-boats in the Irish Sea.

(DECEMBER 1991)

TREFRIW WELLS

Nectar of the Roman legions

MODERN man's quest for alternative medicine has given new life to Trefriw Wells, whose strange-tasting nectar of the Roman gods can now be bought at Harrods. Far better, of course, to seek out the source of the bottled water for yourself, during a quiet journey up the western side of Dyffryn Conwy.

Roman soldiers, marching between their forts at Caerhun and Caer Llugwy, first realised that chalybeate water offered more than mere refreshment. It is not implausible that the Brython inhabitants of Dyffryn Conwy had utilised the water before the arrival of Roman centurions, but it was the latter that excavated three short tunnels to convert the natural springs into shallow wells, which survive to this day.

Whether or not Llywelyn the Great (Llywelyn ap Iorwerth) sampled the iron-impregnated water, we do not know, but he seems to have been the first to appreciate the residential amenities of Trefriw. He founded the local church so as to spare his wife, Joan (daughter of King John of England) the long walk to Llanrhychwyn.

With the passage of time the Roman wells disappeared beneath a landslide and were not re-excavated until 1833. Thirty years later the local landowner, Lord Willoughby de Eresby, built a small two-room bathhouse below the wells. Earthenware pipes fed the water into communal slate baths, one of which is still in situ.

Use of the baths was free until they were closed in 1873, when a private company built the Tudor-style pump room that now stands beside the road, about a mile north of the village to which the wells have given their name. By 1881 the handbook of Trefriw cures, written by a Liverpool doctor, was in its third edition, 'corrected and enlarged,' and covered almost every known disease, commencing with the somewhat modern-sounding 'brain fag'.

'In professional and commercial life mental fag is one of the most prolific causes of derangement of digestion, sanguification and assimilation,' declared the doctor. 'These evils continuing, act and react on each other and increase the disease state until eventually there is induced such a state of atonic congestion of the digestive apparatus and brain as to produce . . . ,' continued the doctor, who then proceeded to list almost every known disease.

His cure was simple: 'The patient should confide his affairs to someone he can trust; he should take with him a friend of congenial spirit and tastes, and a fishing rod and tackle, or a gun and ammunition. He should take up his abode at one of the hotels of Trefriw or Llanrwst; he should retire to bed early at night and rise early in the morning, and he should take a course of Trefriw water.'

It was the golden age of the invalid business, and under the guidance of visionaries like the Reverend Mr Gower, Rector of Trefriw, a bridge was built to link the Spa to Llanrwst railway station. Patients would complete the journey by horse-omnibus for 6d (2½p), or a private cab for half-a-crown (12½p). A paddle-steamer service was also provided from Deganwy and Conwy to the quayside at Trefriw (now cut off from the river by flood prevention embankments). The paddle-steamers were beached south of Conwy bridges in 1939 and eventually scrapped.

Bathrooms were available at the Spa to match one's boat or rail ticket: first class 1s 6d (7½p); second class 1s (5p); and third class 6d (2½p); with an extra 6d all round if one wanted the water warmed. The splendid bathrooms and pump room were smashed with sledgehammers in the 1960s, and hundreds of letters from grateful Victorian aristocracy were burnt, when the building was reduced to a sorry shell before being converted into a house and re-roofed.

One can no longer bathe in Trefriw water but one can look at it for a fee, and buy bottles of it for self-medication.

(JULY 1990)

TREMADOG

Birthplace of Lawrence of Arabia

ONE of Tremadog's shopkeepers replied: 'What for? There is nothing here,' when asked if anyone had ever written a guidebook to this compact gem of early town and country planning. 'Lawrence of Arabia was born down the road,' he added by way of an afterthought.

Originally called Gorphwysfa, and then Woodlands, the home of the Lawrences was labelled Christian Mountain Centre until the late 1990s. That must have confused any Muslims who chanced upon the birthplace of the man who led the Hashemites into the political wilderness in 1917.

There are two small plaques, an older one recording his birth in 1888, and the other affixed a century later by the T.E. Lawrence Society, to mark the planting of a commemorative white-beam tree in the front garden.

Tremadog Town takes its name from its founder, William Alexander Madocks, who reclaimed the necessary land from the tidal estuary of Afon Glaslyn. One enters the delightfully proportioned Market Square via London Street and leaves via Dublin Street, reminding us that Madocks intended it to be a thriving staging post between the two capitals, after the 1801 union of the parliaments of Great Britain and Ireland (to create the United Kingdom).

A proposed new harbour at Porthdinllaen would have eliminated the hazards of sailing from Parkgate, on the Dee, or the frequently fatal coach and ferry journeys across Conwy estuary, Penmaenmawr mountain and the Menai Strait, to Holyhead.

There is yet a third hostelry in the Square, the *Union Inn*, obviously named after the 1801 event, but now mistakenly adorned with the golden lion and red dragon symbols of the 1536 Union of England and Wales, though the lion looks distinctly Scottish.

Now an upmarket shop owned by the Portmeirion family, the old Town Hall remains the focal point of Madocks' plan. In the old Assembly Room, above the ground floor Market Hall, there is a plaque recording that 'Mr Williams-Ellis' (i.e. the eventual Sir Clough, founder of Portmeirion) 'restored and embellished this Hall for its quality and in memory of his mother, Mrs Ellen Mabel Greaves, Tan-y-rallt (sic), who died in 1941 at the age of 90 and was a loyal and lifelong friend of Tremadoc'.

Tan-yr-allt was created in its present form by Madocks, in 1802, on the foundations of an earlier house of the same name. Its most famous tenant was poet Percy B. Shelley, who arrived in 1812 to drum up financial support for Madocks' second embankment, but left in a hurry in 1813 after someone tried to shoot him.

Note, opposite the Town Hall, the slate sign over the Cambrian Pill Depot, established in 1839 by Robert Isaac Jones, in the enlarged house which Madocks had earmarked as the mayor's residence – if his town had ever grown to merit such an appointment.

Much of Madocks' plans could be gleaned from reading memorial plaques in his church, built in Gothic style atop what was a rocky island before he made his first embankment. The beautiful east window was added by the children of another famous owner of Tan-yr-allt and founder of Llechwedd Slate Mines, at Blaenau Ffestiniog. It reads: 'To the glory of God and in loving memory of John Whitehead and Ellen Greaves, this window was erected by their children in 1899.' The inscription has been hidden since World War I behind the reredos, carved and installed by a Belgian refugee named De Vinck. A slate replacement inscription was provided by the family in 1919, at which time Tremadog was part of the archdiocese of Canterbury. No faculty was granted for its installation and it became forgotten until I found it, hidden behind a pew, in 1990. Two years later the Church in Wales granted a faculty for a smaller replacement plaque to be affixed to one of the church walls. The church was closed in 1999.

(AUGUST 1990)

TREMEIRCHION

Less than Dr Johnson expected

TREMEIRCHION is best known for its association with Samuel Johnson, an event recorded in the church with a plaque stating: 'Near this place lies buried Hester Lynch Piozzi, Dr Johnson's Mrs Thrale, born 1741, died 1821.' The plaque was installed in 1909 by the grandson of her executor Sir James Fellowes.

Born at Bodfel, near Pwllheli, she was the daughter of John Salusbury, of Bachygraig, Tremeirchion. Her mother was of the Cotton family who, one hundred and seventy-four years later, established the Women's Institute in Britain, at Llanfair Pwllgwyngyll.

It was to a dilapidated Bachygraig that she introduced Dr Johnson in 1774, when she and her husband, Streatham brewer Henry Thrale, took him on his famous tour of north Wales. 'The floors have been stolen; the windows are stopped. The house was less than I seemed to expect,' recorded Johnson on 30 July. 'Far worse than I expected,' noted Mrs Thrale in her diary.

Hester Salusbury first married in 1763. She was widowed in 1781 and lost the friendship of Johnson and others of her London set in 1784, when she decided to marry Italian music teacher Gabriel Piozzi, a Roman Catholic. As Mrs Piozzi she returned to the family seat which she had inherited, and although some repair work was done to Bachygraig she and her husband built a house which they called Brynbella – a mixture of Welsh and Italian into which they moved in 1795.

The elegant Italianate house still stands, its main lodge and ornately gilded iron gates being in the village, but its long term future became uncertain with the death of its widowed nonagenarian owner in 1993. Much of Bachygraig also stands, now a farmhouse. It was built in 1567-69 for Sir Richard Clough, whose initials still remain, but the main residential block was demolished in 1817. Clough's financial influence on Antwerp was reciprocated in the Dutch architectural influence on Bachygraig.

While there is no problem finding the graves of the rest of the Salusbury family, mystery surrounds the whereabouts of authoress Hester Piozzi and her husband. The local folk memory says their grave was obliterated by the northern transept added to the medieval church in 1864.

The church is full of interest, including the ornate altar tomb inscribed, in Latin: 'Here lies David, son of Hywel, son of Madog', this being Dafydd Ddu o Hiraddug, the 14th century incumbent who produced the first Welsh translation from the Book of Psalms.

More intriguing is the figure of a knight in armour, reset in the wall of the Victorian transept. Once part of an altar tomb, and resembling a crusader, the heraldry on his shield is said to identify the figure as Sir Robert Pounderling, a 12th century constable of Dyserth castle.

The windows in the chancel are in memory of Harriet, wife of the Revd William Hicks Owen who was the Vicar here for an incredible fifty-seven years. Mrs Owen's music is still played in the church. She was a sister of Felicia Hemans, author of *The Boy Stood on the Burning Deck*. All three lived together at Rhyllon, at nearby Waen.

The church is flanked on one side by the 1865 school, and on the other by the ancient Salusbury Arms, which is equipped with an organ for evening entertainment.

(DECEMBER 1993)

WAUNFAWR

Where Marconi reigned

WAUNFAWR was once the world's most important radio centre, transmitting the word of the overgrown British Empire to the upstart United States. Something of its past glory is still to be found at Cefn Du, the much-quarried mountain that rises above the straggling village to a height of 1,449 feet (440m).

It was the opening of the slate quarry, in 1800, which created the village of Waunfawr. At its peak it employed two hundred men but went into liquidation in 1928. A Presbyterian chapel, once with a couple of outstations, and an Anglican church built in 1880, remind us of Waunfawr's heyday.

The big empty garage in the village centre is fondly remembered as the depot of Waunfawr's very own fleet of fifteen Whiteways buses, founded in 1911 by Owen R. Williams, and closed in 1989 by his 88-years-old son Robert Glyn Williams.

Guglielmo Marconi arrived in the village in 1914, to build a massive transmitter hall, 83 ft (25m) high, and 100 ft (30m) long, which now provides stabling for Plas-y-celyn trekking and riding centre. Variously known as Waunfawr, Waenfawr, Cefn Du, Wales Transoceanic or Caernarvon Radio Station, it was designed to broadcast Morse messages to Belmar, New Jersey.

The first transatlantic radio signal was heard in 1900, at St John's, Newfoundland. It was the letter S (three dots in Morse) which was being transmitted continuously from an aerial suspended by a kite at Poldhu, in Cornwall. Encouraged by a Canadian government subsidy, Marconi had built a transmitter at Clifden, on the western shores of Ireland, in 1907, but quickly recognised the need for a more convenient link with the bigger market offered by the United States.

He chose Waunfawr for his new station and installed a 300 kW transmitter, to broadcast on a cumbersome long-wave inverted L aerial suspended from ten 400 ft (122m) high masts, in two rows 250 ft (76m) apart. The usual operating wavelength was 10,000 metres.

In those days transmitters and receivers had to be separated by at least 40 miles (65km) for simultaneous working, and the answering signals from New Brunswick, USA, were first received at Tywyn, Meirionnydd. The problem of tuning out one's own transmitter was solved soon afterwards and Waunfawr also became a wartime listening station, intercepting signals from Stavanger – the results being sent to the War Office by train, from Caernarfon, every morning.

Many historic broadcasts were made from Waunfawr, including a much-publicised 'first signal heard in the Antipodes' in 1918. It was a Morse signal from William Morris Hughes, the Welsh Prime Minister of Australia, pleading for more volunteers for the war in Flanders. It was not quite the first signal, however, for Waunfawr engineers had spent many weeks experimenting with nightly transmissions of the Ten Commandments, so as to make sure the Premier's message would be heard in Sydney by the Amalgamated Wireless Company of Australia.

The first radio transmission of a photograph, the Derby winner, was made from Waunfawr in 1927, after months of experiments in high-speed signalling by the local second-engineer. Six new masts and the more efficient short-wave system had been installed by GEC for Cable & Wireless Ltd in 1923, but the station closed early in 1939, and all 16 masts were removed as scrap metal by Thomas Ward, of Sheffield, for reuse in making war weapons.

The last Marconi employee, by then working as a site caretaker for the GPO, successors in the post-war nationalisation of Cable & Wireless, was Hughie Jones, who was pensioned off in 1961, when he was 69 years of age. He had spent forty-six years on the site, and much of the information in this feature is derived from records he showed me when he retired.

Antique ceramic insulators high up on one of the walls of the old transmitter hall are the only surviving relics of its radio days. The 70-ton concrete anchor points for the mast-supporting stays also remain in situ.

(DECEMBER 1991)

WHITFORD

Thomas Pennant's home

WHITFORD was the home of the greatest of all Welsh travel writers, Thomas Pennant, whose *Tours in Wales*, published in two volumes in 1778 and 1781, is still a popular seller.

The village name was derived from a swift-flowing little river (Afon Dre-Lan) which formed a white ford before it was culverted long, long ago. The Welsh translation would be 'rhyd wen', which would make a perfectly good place name.

However bilingual boundary signs tell us we have arrived at Chwitffordd, which is nothing more than a colloquial mispronunciation of the English – albeit one that has spanned at least seven centuries. Called Widford in the Domesday Book of 1086, it was corrupted to Chwitforth by 1284 and amended to the present Welsh spelling as long ago as 1550.

No longer on the road to anywhere that is not served by a better alternative, Whitford has little through traffic and is altogether a peaceful place – which is just as well, with parking at a premium except for patrons of the village pub. Now called The Huntsman, its facade has been spoilt by the addition of a pseudo-crenellated stone porch. Older residents still call it the

Mostyn Arms, reminding us that Mostyn Estate has a backdoor into the village, via the strangely-named Pennsylvania Lodge. Bedrooms at the Mostyn Arms were used as temporary classrooms after the village church school was destroyed by fire in the 1920s.

Downing was the other big estate, where Thomas Pennant was born in 1726, and where he died 72 years later. Built in 1627, the house was altered by Thomas Pennant in 1766, by his son in 1814, and by his great grand-daughter (the Countess of Denbigh) in 1858. At the turn of the last century Downing was the home of Sir William Tate, of Tate & Lyle sugar. Alas the house was destroyed by fire in 1922 and the ruins were demolished in 1953. All that is left is a fragment of wall beside a shallow pond, in an area reclaimed by indigenous trees. The stable block, bearing the date 1766, still stands, and part of it is in use as a rented house.

Pennant was buried inside the parish church, where a rather fine white marble memorial is partly obscured by the organ console. The church's most famous organist was Charles Smart, of the BBC, who evacuated himself to Upper Downing in 1940, and frequently gave recitals in the church.

Using the natural slope of the land, the church interior has a raked floor, so that even those at the back have a full view of the altar. With an ancient north nave (now used as an aisle) and an early Victorian nave, there is plenty of wall space for plaques to the good and the great of Whitford. A window commemorates Major-General Sir Savage Mostyn of the Royal Welch Fusiliers, the man who gave the Great Orme its feral herd of Royal Kashmir goats.

Moses Griffith, who illustrated Pennant's best-known book, is buried in the churchyard, near the northern boundary wall, where local enthusiasts are preparing a place for a Welsh plaque to supplement the English inscription on his original tombstone of 1818.

The churchyard is unusual in having two lych gates, one

now used for weddings and the other for funerals. The former has a neat little room over the archway, bearing a plaque stating that £5 was left towards its construction in 1624.

(SEPTEMBER 1992)

Y GRAIG

Organ in the valley

Y GRAIG, in Dyffryn Conwy, was bypassed by the Llanrwst Turnpike Trust in 1837, after which there was no need for anyone to enter the hamlet if heading anywhere else – a fact which remains true to this day. Miraculously, the breeze-block and beamless roof brigade of modern developers has also bypassed this community of some twenty houses, in which I spent much of my childhood. Three pairs of semi-detached houses were added early this century, since when development has been more or less confined to discreet modernisation.

I knew Y Graig when it boasted two shops, a bakehouse and a dairy – the latter alongside the communal well, now filled up in the garden of Tŷ Lawr. The hamlet's water source gave its name to Well Street, once a terrace of four cottages, but now converted into two. No. 3 Well Street was the home of Wil Goetre, who one day took himself off to Liverpool to buy a spanking new chapel organ for his cottage. The console took up most of his living room, the bellows filled the kitchen, and the pipes passed through the ceiling. His hymn tunes periodically shattered the peace of the valley, and are among my strongest childhood memories. He died about half-a-century ago and his organ went to a farm in Bryn-y-maen.

Wil Goetre's intrusive hymns were the nearest Y Graig ever got to having a chapel, for the nonconformist building frenzy of the Victorian era passed it by – perhaps fooled by the 1837 bypass. Worship came a little more discreetly, by way of a

Sunday school above the shop of Pryce Hughes, or Siop Ucha, still identifiable though now converted into a house. 'Weekday services were also held there, as well as concerts and eisteddfodau, and it was there we learnt to read in Welsh,' recalled Miss Elizabeth Lloyd, who was born in 1903. She recalled open air summer services on the rock (which gives the community its name) opposite Pryce Hughes's shop. 'I remember uniformed soldiers joining in when on leave during the first World War,' she added.

More imagination is needed to identify Siop Isa, on the opposite corner from Siop Ucha. A plastic butterfly on the wall is attached to the slab on which one used to read: 'J.W. Jones, Flour and Coal Merchant'. This was the shop and bakery patronised by my grandmother, a giant of a woman still remembered as 'Mrs Jones, plysmon', not for her own attempts to police Y Graig, but as a policeman's widow who had retired to her native patch, having been born at nearby Glanconwy.

John Jones, Siop Isa, owned a horse and trap with which he delivered coal on Tuesdays, Wednesdays and Fridays, and bread on Mondays, Thursdays and Saturdays – the latter baked not with coal but with gorse harvested off the surrounding hillsides. His wife Esther ran the shop, dressed in layers of voluminous skirts, and never without a hat. As well as groceries she kept the community supplied with paraffin for lighting and cooking.

Electricity did not reach Y Graig until 1952, and a year later everyone piled into No. 4 Y Graig to watch the community's first television set, installed by Mrs Pritchard for the Coronation of Queen Elizabeth II.

'Apart from meat, which came with a travelling butcher, the two shops supplied most of our needs,' recalled Y Graig's oldest inhabitant, Mrs Annie Jones, 87. 'The shops also mixed medicines for us from a collection of bottles – few of us could afford to pay for a doctor,' she added.

(JUNE 1992)

YSBYTY IFAN

A Crusader village

YSBYTY IFAN is a name to conjure with, taking us straight back to the Crusades and the Knights Hospitaller of the Order of St John of Jerusalem. Close to the source of Afon Conwy, it was known as Dolgynwal (Cynwal's meadow) until 1190, when it was given the Latin mantle of *Hospitium Iohannes*, meaning John's Hospital in English, or Ysbyty IEVAN/Ieuan/Ifan in Welsh (the later 'Ioan' version of *Iohannes* was adopted for the 16th century Welsh Bible).

Impressed by Archbishop Baldwin and his Welsh interpreter Giraldus Cambrensis, when they toured these parts in 1188, recruiting three thousand Welshmen for the Crusades, local nobleman Ifan ap Rhys, of Plasiolyn, Pentrefoelas, gave land for the Knights Hospitaller to set up a branch at Dolgynwal.

The Order of St John was founded in Jerusalem in 1099, by knights who adopted an ancient pilgrims' hospice close to Helen's original Church of the Holy Sepulchre. Jerusalem's hospice is now no more than a plaque on a wall, but several medieval relics of the Ysbyty Ifan branch have survived into the present St John's church, built in 1861. They include alabaster effigies of: (1) Rhys Fawr ap Meredydd, of Plas Iolyn, dating from about 1483, showing him in armour covered with a tabard, and wearing a chain and crucifix; (2) his wife Lowri; and (3) his son Robert ap Rhys, circa 1536, shown in monastic dress.

Rhys Fawr was Henry VII's standard bearer at the Battle of Bosworth; Robert ap Rhys was chaplain to Cardinal Wolsey and lessee of Ysbyty Ifan manor at the dissolution of the smaller monasteries in 1536 – when the hospice became the parish church. The church also contains the memorial to Robert and Ann Gethin, of nearby Cernioge, who died within a month of each other in 1598.

In 1970 Dr Ifor Davies, of Cerrigydrudion (whose

grandfather lies buried in the churchyard at Ysbyty Ifan) wrote to Denbighshire County Council, suggesting the church's links with the Order of St John should be commemorated with a stained glass window. He was, alas, dead by the time his dream came true, nearly a quarter of a century later.

The Duchess of Gloucester, Commandant-in-Chief of the Order's Ambulance Brigade in Wales, joined the congregation on 18 September 1993 for the dedication of the window which visitors can now see in the north wall. The event marked the 75th anniversary of the founding of the Priory for Wales of the Most Venerable Order of the Hospital of St John of Jerusalem. (The story of the links between Ysbyty Ifan and Jerusalem is told in the commemorative book *The Order of St John in Wales*, by Ivor Wynne Jones, 1993).

Ysbyty Ifan's oldest surviving house is dated 1774, at the centre of a terrace extended on either side, perhaps half-a-century later. A clue as to why all the houses are so well built, to an obvious development plan, is to be found in the simple inscription 'Ffynnon Penrhyn, 1866' beside the approach road, reminding us that this was once part of the Penrhyn Estate – founded on African slaves, Caribbean sugar and Bethesda slate.

There is a robust corn mill on the right as one approaches the narrow humpbacked bridge, with its water wheel intact at the rear though it has not turned for several decades. Adapting to the changing agricultural pattern of Cynwal's meadow, the grandson of the original miller installed a turbine in 1945 and supplied the hundred inhabitants with electricity until the Merseyside and North Wales Electricity Board turned up twenty years later. During the whole of that time he never increased his charge of thirty shillings (£1.50) a year, for a maximum of four lamps per cottage.

The hamlet's architectural heritage is badly let down by the Memorial Hall, rebuilt in 1958 to replace the hall destroyed by fire in 1940, while used as a barracks for a Royal Artillery searchlight unit – seeking German bombers on their way to

Liverpool. However the Memorial Hall earned fame in 1978 when used as Katherine Hepburn's base for the filming, at Ysbyty Ifan, of Emlyn Williams's *The Corn is Green*.

(OCTOBER 1991)

FURTHER READING

Further information about some of the places and topics touched upon in this book may be found in other titles by Ivor Wynne Jones, more especially:

Shipwrecks of North Wales (1973, 1978, 1986, 2001)

Llandudno, Queen of the Welsh resorts (1975)

Colwyn Bay, a brief history (1995)

Betws-y-coed and the Conwy Valley (1974)

Money for all: the story of the Welsh pound (1969)

The Order of St John in Wales (1993)

Gold, Frankenstein and manure (1997)

The Llechwedd Strike of 1893 (1993)

Alice's Welsh Wonderland (1999)

Fort Belan (1979)